Oh Crap - I'm 50!

A Journey from Fearful to Fabulous (Sometimes)

Jo Blackwell

2

This book is dedicated to
everyone who followed and took part in project50,
to my family, who bore their ruthless exploitation with patience
and good humour,
and to anyone who pauses at the time of their 50th birthday and
thinks:
what now?

INTRODUCTION

When I was a kid in the long-forgotten sixties and seventies, 50 was old. It probably still is to kids today, but those of us who have reached that milestone birthday know that it's different from our mothers' and fathers' day. The old certainties such as jobs for life, pay off your mortgage by 50, safe pensions, may have been swept away, but so have our previous limiting expectations of ourselves, perpetuated in the media by ads for incontinence pads, funeral plans and gentle cruises.

My husband once told me we were like a pair of comfortable slippers. I think he thought he was being romantic. Sorry, darling, but to hell with THAT - I'm still a pair of f**k me stilettos! (Albeit whilst wearing orthopaedic insoles).

When I started the blog, **project50** in 2010, I was feeling old, unfit, overweight and cast aside. Throw in hormonal upheavals, multiple bereavements, financial catastrophe and an emptying nest and I can honestly say it was one of the darkest times I have ever experienced.

My rapidly approaching 50th birthday was the icing on the bitter cake. I figured there must be others "out there" who felt the same way as me. Reaching out and connecting was the best thing I have ever done for it brought me new friends, a new career and a much happier, more hopeful future.

Project50 consisted of articles, personal commentary, music, poetry and words of wisdom from those much wiser than me, plus interviews and photographs of other 50-somethings. For a year I posted almost every day, then intermittently for a further 12 months.

It has been a pleasure to revisit the blog eight years later and choose the posts for inclusion. Reading back, it is clear that the first year was a howl in the dark. In the second year the posts gradually become more hopeful until, finally, they tail away as I spent more time living and less time thinking about it.

DISCLAIMER

I'm not a celebrity, nor am I an "expert" on ageing (or anything else for that matter!) I am an English, middle-aged wife, mother and grandmother. I earn a crust by making images and writing. I am "not a *practical* person" as my mother suggested recently, but I am a thinker, and we need all sorts in this world, don't we? I believe my experience of life is as valid as any household name's, as is yours. My aim is primarily to entertain you - I can't be held responsible if you laugh out loud on the train or decide to jack in your job to fulfil your lifelong ambition to bungee jump around the world. I hope you'll write and tell me all about it, though!

All best,

THE BEGINNING

Today I enter my fiftieth year. Does that make me…
OVER THE HILL…?

A new grey hair each week and ever-deepening wrinkles, failing eyesight – a blessing since it means I can't see the former so clearly in the morning mirror – and creaking knees that bend but can't be relied upon to straighten again. An empty nest, (now they've gone, what exactly am I for?) and a growing realisation that this is it: the rehearsal is well and truly over.

It always was, of course, but knowing that more of my life is in my past than in my future is a sobering thought.

I'd rectify that if my liver hadn't given up the ghost ten years ago. Half a glass of wine and I'm drunk. An hour later I'm hungover. One of the last things my father said to me before he checked out at 58 was: "Life's a bitch and then you die." Thanks, Dad.

Bette Davis famously said that ageing isn't for sissies. But I *am* a sissy! I'm a paid up member of the English Suburban Sissy Club – if they had badges I'd have earned my nth degree of sissy-dom. I'd be a Patrol Leader.

Getting older is a bit like childbirth: there's no changing your mind, no going back, no matter how much you yell or swear or rage against the dying of the light. No amount of corsetry or face cream can save you.

The illusion that we have an element of control over our lives is exposed as the sham it always was, so we might as well face it head on. Is that the essence of that old cliche, the midlife crisis? That we start to let go and roll with what life throws at us?

Or ... **ON TOP OF THE WORLD?**

So the kids have gone (along with most of my money). I'm fortunate enough not to have elderly parents to care for since I'm unfortunate enough to have lost at least one. Suddenly, my time is my own. Husband of my heart has his own routines – work, gym, cricket, sport on TV – I can now read a book from beginning to end without interruption. No one wakes me in the night because they're hungry of they've wet the bed (not even husband). No one calls me from A & E in the middle of the night because they've "tripped on an uneven pavement" and smashed their nose on the way out of a club.

I could eat a whole box of chocolates whilst watching American Idol, lying on the sofa in the nude if I so wanted. (If my window cleaner's reading this, it's ok, Eddie, that was just an imaginary scenario). I can dance, if I really want to, or sing at the top of my lungs and no one's going to roll their eyes.

Looking around me, I see so many people whose lives are falling apart at 50 – divorce, unemployment, bereavement, illness – and so many, often the same people, who live their lives with energy, optimism and enthusiasm. I sense that 50 could be fun... if I let it be so!

Over the past year, I've re-trained as a photographer and am slowly building my business, specialising in portraiture. I never expected to discover something new about myself that would give me so much pleasure. I feel a growing urge to connect with ... well, people like you!

And I'm having a blast, looking for and meeting interesting folk to interview, talking to radio DJs and magazine editors and generally spreading the word about project50. Maybe it's not so bad...

BITTERSWEET

My empty nest was populated again this weekend as two of my four children – the boys – came home for my birthday. One arrived with wife and little sons in tow, so from a household of two we became seven and chaos reigned like a happy echo from the not so distant past.

Both my boys are so tall they can count the grey hairs on top of my head now – and take great delight in doing so. I am so proud of the men they have become, men I like and whose company I enjoy. And yet, and yet…

How I miss the sensitive, thoughtful little boy who once told me he'd worked out the meaning of life (for us all to love and help each other, just in case you're wondering) and the sharp-witted, serious child who questioned everyone and everything around him, trusting nothing until he'd investigated it himself.

I can still feel the imprint of their little hands in mine, still recall the smell of their freshly washed hair and the feel of small arms around my neck as, freshly pyjama-ed, I carried them to bed. The countless hours I spent answering endless questions, repeatedly reading well-loved stories, ferrying to and from from school, to parties, matches, guitar lessons, play dates, A & E – like every mother, that was my life.

It was, of course, a life lived in a general fog of exhaustion – the look in my daughter-in-law's eyes reminded me of that part – but the memory of that fades, leaving only the gold-tinted remembrance of family unity.

So my sons breezed in with their hugs and loud voices and frequent bursts of laughter and I was enveloped once again by their easy, boisterous love. My daughters phoned, wistfully, from London and Cornwall, my grandsons, one almost four, the other nine months old, filled the house with the urgent demands of the young and for two blissful days I found myself busy once more with kindergarten conversation and infant games.

And then a flurry of hugs and hasty last-minute conversation and they were gone, spiralling away like two Catherine wheels to opposite ends of the country, leaving the house devastated, quiet and still.

Husband of my heart has cleared the garden chairs and parasol and has retreated to the hammock. A battered football lies forgotten by the vegetable patch. A familiar, dull ache of loss throbs in the pit of my stomach.

My aim always was to nurture happy, confident children, the end result of which are strong, independent adults who are able to leave the nest with barely a backward glance. So I am, I guess, a victim of my own success and, in truth, would not really want them to be living in my pocket. I am conscious of my good luck at having had my children, and for the fact that they remember my birthday at all.

They love me and their father. They love each other and will return, periodically, to revisit and renew the bonds of childhood. I am so fortunate for that, and for the daughters and sons-in-law and grandchildren that are beginning to arrive. I know I am still part of their lives, and am grateful, even while I know that the days when I was at their centre are gone for good. I accept it and let them go with my blessing. However, they are at my centre still. Therein lies the source of my grief as I contemplate my empty nest – I miss them.

LETTER TO MY DAUGHTERS

So, my bright, brave, beautiful girls, has the title of this post got you quaking? Worried what your mother's going to make public? You might be horrified that the whole world is now exposed to the "mum-isms" that embarrass you so much (such as my off the cuff remark on the radio on Friday about being top heavy with men), but actually most people don't take me that seriously.

No, this is my way of imparting my priceless pearls of wisdom across the miles, sent with love (and only a little devilment!) You'll have heard some of it before, but it bears saying again. Some of it will apply to you, some won't, but I've lived a little, so this is hard-won intel here. Pay attention.

So, as you go through life as the strong, independent young women that you are, please remember the following:

- You are beautiful. Believe it. You'll know it's true in thirty years when you look at old photographs and remember how you hated your nose/chin/thighs, whatever, by which time it's too late to enjoy being young and gorgeous.

- Life is too short to spend it worrying. Apart from a little light long-term planning, take each day as it comes and roll with the punches.

- Never, ever say *"that's just my luck"* when something bad happens, or it will be, trust me.

- Always take responsibility for your own health. If you eat lard you'll get fat. Smoke too much, you'll drop dead. Drink too much, you'll wake up with your knickers on your head.

- Never be afraid to wake up with your knickers on your head. It shows character.

- But try not to wake up with someone else's underwear about your person.

- The best contraception known to woman is the word *"no"*. If you can't remember that you'll never remember to take a daily pill.

- Find something to laugh at **EVERY SINGLE DAY**

- When life gets tough, try to stay cheerful. A long face gets slapped more often than a smiley one. Plus frowning will mean all your wrinkles will point downwards.

- Nothing lasts forever, bad or good. Accept that and you'll appreciate what is.

- In the Western world, Life is rarely as hard or as complicated as most people perceive it to be. Keep it simple.

- Cultivate *"an attitude of gratitude"*

- Remember where you came from, but never, ever look back.

- Except to say hello to your parents every now and then.

- Don't labour under the illusion that you have to phone me every day. I have a life. But you are still a huge and much loved part of it, so try to fit in a weekly call.

- Always listen to your intuition - better to be safe and look an arse than sorry and fall on yours.

- Believe in yourself - you are without a doubt two of the brightest, most precious souls currently gracing this planet. And I am not biased.

- Stay interested in life. It is very interesting.

- Always looks for the good in people - there are more good people in this world than bad. Most are simply doing their best to get by, just like you.

- Never say *"I'm not a feminist, but…"* The basic definition of a feminist is a woman who values herself. That's it.

- Always listen to advice respectfully, but never feel obliged to take it. Not even mine.

- Stand by your own decisions and own your triumphs as well as your failures

- Be frugal with money. Strive to want what you have, rather than have what you want.

- Never miss an opportunity to help someone else.

- Always be kind.

- Remember, how you feel is a matter of choice. Choose to be happy.

That's all the wisdom of my years distilled into a few hundred words. As you know, I don't always manage to live this way, but I do try. At the end of the day, in the words of the song, the love you take is equal to the love you make, so make sure you make lots of love. Er... maybe I'd better stop there, girls. Wouldn't want to embarrass you.

Love Mum xx

HAS ANYONE SEEN MY MEMORY?

I know I put it down somewhere…

My kids call it the Mum-dance. It's a ritual that takes place every time I leave the house and involves yours truly darting backwards and forwards looking for keys, purse, glasses and a final check that I've remembered to put on my shoes.

One of the most irritating – and most anxiety-inducing – aspects of middle age is the changes that appear to take place in the brain as we age. The words that escape you, the names that won't appear: these are signs of the slowing down of memory and reaction times. There is also some evidence that older people take longer to learn new things and that, worryingly, are more likely to make mistakes than when they were younger. So what's the good news?

Well, a recent study in the US has found that, contrary to the received wisdom that brain cells die off with age and aren't replaced, in fact brain cells continue to grow, meaning that there is no reason why the middle-aged brain can't absorb new information. Better still, another US study has shown that it's possible to increase the plasticity – or adaptability – of the brain through physical exercise. (Note to off-spring: that "Mum-dance" has a real-world application)

The good news continues as researchers have found that complex reasoning skills actually improve in middle age, meaning that we grasp and anticipate problems better than ever. We also become more empathetic with age, understanding and connecting with other people more easily.

Barbara Strauch, in her book, *The Secret Life of the Grown-up Brain: The Surprising Talents of the Middle-Aged Mind*, claims that much of the memory loss we believe to be inevitable is simply down to bad habits and expectation.

A 2009 study showed that white matter in the brain increases with age, peaking in mid-life, and that, contrary to earlier scientific findings, white matter is more important than the grey when it comes to utilising information. Wisdom could therefore be explained by the older brain's facility for assessing a situation quickly and accurately and its ability to make cool, measured decisions.

It would seem, then, that we can all look forward to many more years of active brain function. Just remember that, like anything else, if you don't want to lose it, you need to use it! Now, where did I put those glasses...

2018 Note: *Our knowledge on neuroplasticity has come on in leaps and bounds since I wrote this and the science is fascinating*

THE INVISIBLE WOMAN

I am beginning to wonder if I am invisible. I checked in the mirror this morning, in fact, (I've seen those films where the main character thinks they're being haunted and it turns out that no, they ARE the ghost!) but I appeared to be all present and correct.

Husband of my heart confirmed it when he rolled over and said "your turn to make the tea." He wouldn't say that if I wasn't really there, would he? Unless he's a ghost too...

Anyway, there have been several incidents recently that have led me to this worrying conclusion. The first was in Hyde Park a couple of weeks ago at the Paul McCartney concert (more of which later) when I was literally trodden on several times.

The crowd was enormous and I was there, in the middle, about eight heaving rows from the front. Luckily, having arrived early doors, I was completely oblivious to the enormity of the audience, or I think I might have had a panic attack (which just proves that my perceived fear of crowds really is all in the mind).

It was a great line-up, including Elvis Costello and Crosby, Stills and Nash, but it involved standing, on one of the hottest days in London this summer, for approximately 11 hours. So I tried to pace myself a bit by sitting down between acts. Problem was, as the hour of Sir Paul's appearance neared, the crowd kept surging forward and packing itself tighter and tighter.

I had toes insinuated beneath my buttocks (and not in a pleasant way) when I was sitting, elbows driven into my ribs when I was standing, on one occasion a girl actually crashed into me and would have knocked me off my feet if there had been somewhere for me to fall. If it wasn't for Son No.2 standing firm behind me, I would have been manoeuvred to the margins well before the end of the gig. Thanks to him, I was able to at least bend my knees in time to the music and had room for my (not insubstantial) chest to rise and fall as I sang along to "Hey Jude".

When it was time for me to leave, Daughter No.1 had to grasp me by the wrist and drag me along behind her for fear of losing me in the heaving, now mobile crowd all heading for the last Tube home.

It happened when I was boarding a flight last month. Caught in an EasyJet melee, my family were all seated, belted and plugged into iPods before I even got through the plane door.

On Friday night it was Son No.1's turn to protect me from dance floor revellers as we watched The Beavers in a function suite in Stockport. That crowd was considerably more amiable than some of Sir Paul's so-called fans, but still I found myself being edged further and further back until, before I knew it, I was in a stranger's lap (but I was invisible, so luckily she didn't notice).

I asked my husband about it. "Who said that?" he replied with some alarm.

I clearly don't have a presence, an aura about me that says, "Here I am – I have a right to be here, so back off!" Maybe I'm too polite, too English, too self-effacing? Too short? Psychologically timid? Lacking energy? Whatever it is, it's beginning to hack me off.

Just as an aside, you remember I told you that the McCartney concert took place in 31 degree heat? I was so squashed I couldn't get to my bag to reapply sunscreen. Consequently, my careful, if doomed preservation of my face went to pot for a day. So you could say that Paul McCartney gave me freckles. Only it doesn't matter because I'm invisible.

WHOSE HANDS?

I could write reams about the sadness I feel at the slow, but relentless degradation of my body. I shall skim over the details lest it put you off your skinny latte, suffice it to say that I now have more curves than angles and about as much spring-back-ability in my skin as a piece of broken knicker elastic.

I've changed my mind – have a few details:

I now have what I like to call "silver highlights", though who I think would actually sit in the hairdresser's with foils on their head to achieve this effect I have no idea. Over time, my foundation wear (what a lovely, old-fashioned phrase!) has become more about containment and less about boasting and I sometimes find myself hunting for "comfortable" knickers. You know, ladies, the kind that your grandmother told you would "keep your kidneys warm".

Failing eyesight helps, of course. I was sitting in the garden with my daughter last summer and casually remarked (as you do) that I was saving a fortune on waxing as the hair on my legs just doesn't seem to grow as fast any more. She raised an eloquent eyebrow at me. "Go and get your glasses, Mum," she advised. OMG! as I would have to say if I was texting

Speaking of legs, mine, I have to report, do not like being parted for long. I ill-advisedly went horse-riding a year ago and after an hour in the saddle my hips had frozen into position so that I couldn't dismount. I had to be lifted – quite literally – from the saddle by a stablehand and placed, deformed and agonised, on a mounting block. I hasten to add that the stablehand then walked away – this is not that kind of story. Besides, these days, in the bedroom, I am less likely to cry out in passion than I am in pain as I am convulsed with cramp.

But these trials are as nothing when I catch a glimpse of my hands. It's as if a malevolent gnome has crept into my room at night, armed with liposuction equipment and sucked out all the fat on my fingers. My fingers, you stupid bloody gnomes – didn't you read the training manual? You're welcome to the fat in my thighs, I needed the stuff in my fingers! My knuckles have grown baggy, the backs of my hands wrinkle at the slightest touch and I go through hand cream the way the England football team go through excuses.

I would like to kid myself that I am beyond such vanity, that I actually like the way my eyes disappear like shy currants when I laugh. "Every wrinkle tells a story", my grandmother used to say. Bollocks. Every wrinkle makes me less recognisable to myself!

Seriously, do I really, really care? On one level, yes I do, if I'm honest. Sure, there are far worse tragedies that have befallen me, let alone wider humanity, than the marks of age which are arriving thick and fast. I wish I wasn't so shallow that I could see beyond my poor old hands in a photo to the happy smile that generally accompanies half a glass of wine (my limit).

At least my wrinkles mostly curve upward: a legacy of keeping a smile on my face even through the darkest times. And on another level, there are far too many more interesting things to occupy my mind than how I look. It's not as if other people notice much - becoming invisible in middle age is not such a bad thing! Nor is failing eyesight.

If I don't look too closely, I barely notice. I guess that's the answer to the "problem" - I think I'll turn my attention to more interesting things!

LETTER TO MY SISTER

Dear Sal,

I've been your sister now for nearly 44 years and you STILL don't listen to me, so I thought I'd write you a letter instead. You've always been a bit annoying (which is why I used to shut you in the cupboard when we were small) but lovable and so, so kind, which is why I keep nagging you.

What do I keep nagging you about? I knew you weren't listening when I saw you today! I want to get hold of you and shake you because you deserve to see your dreams come true. You work so hard at so many different jobs, always running at full tilt just to stand still. I want you to take a breath and see the possibilities that surround you. I don't think you realise how much I admire you. We are so different in our skills and interests, but we are both creative in our own ways.

When you were younger you never sat still for a minute. Dad's lodger used to called you *"whoosh-whoosh"* because you'd whoosh in and whoosh out again like a human tornado, leaving everybody breathless. Since you met Mark and settled down and had your lovely girl you've mellowed. You've become the "you" that you were always meant to be… almost.

I say "almost" because you seem to be afraid to follow your dreams. I'm talking about the catering company you could so easily start, or the cleaning business you could run, the craft business in which you would do so well, the cake-making that would pay your bills on its own and the small-holding you long to develop.

It's as if you think that these ideas are too grand for you, that such things are for other people, not you. And they will be, if you don't bite the bullet and start making a plan. How much money do other people make from your hard work? That money should be yours, for you to become the Sally you deserve to be.

Don't get me wrong: you're lovely as you are. I just think you could be enjoying your life more if you weren't constantly sweating for other people who don't appreciate you as they should.

I know you have commitments and things are tight. I know that it's scary to even think about changing things. But isn't it even scarier to race towards your fifties in a fog of exhaustion with all these wonderful ideas of yours locked away inside you?

It's like eating healthily. You're always saying that you want to lose weight, that this food doesn't suit you, or that food makes you tired. So what's stopping you? Don't you want to feel better? To have the energy to live your life? What is it that's holding you back?

It all boils down to looking after YOU, doesn't it? Like so many mothers, you're brilliant at looking after your family, your friends, your community, but pretty shit at looking after you. Look at all the help you've given me as I start my business.

So start thinking of yourself as a friend who needs nurturing and believe in yourself. Walt Disney said: "If we can dream it, we can do it." And that's the point, Sal – you're not alone. As soon as you start generating that positive energy around you, you'll be amazed at how things fall into place. Start small, dream big.

Take one small step, half a step even. Or I'll have to shut you in a cupboard. Again.

With love, always,

your Big Sis

50 WAYS TO FLOURISH AT 50
Numbers 1-5

Exercise regularly, but listen carefully to your body. For example, if you have incipient arthritis in your knees, pounding the pavements is pointless, counter-productive and probably painful. Sports like golf must have been invented for a reason.

Walk. The simplest way to maintain a basic level of fitness and mobility is to walk briskly for 30 minutes a day for 5 days a week. Try marching 15 minutes from your doorstep before turning back before breakfast. Not only will you reduce your risk of heart attack and obesity, it will lift your spirits, especially if you can walk somewhere green.

Your joints might start to ache, but you can largely determine how much they ache by choosing good nutrition and exercise. Ditto your weight. Own the consequences of your choices.

If you have serious health challenges, reach out for support and try to focus on what you *can* do, rather than mourn for what you *can't*.

Stretching every morning and evening is no longer an choice if you want to stay supple.
Better still, practice Yoga or Pilates

WE OVER 50s ARE HOT!

No, really – we're HOT! You see us everywhere, stripping off when everyone else is in puffa jackets, fanning ourselves with concert programmes, edging surreptitiously towards oscillating fans whilst trying to continue with our conversations. And no, guys, it isn't because you've moved into our orbit. Sorry.

If you're not menopausal, close your eyes and imagine a wave of warm air rolling across your skin. Pleasant, huh? Now turn up the heat – go on, high enough so that you break into a sweat – and feel that wave turn into a tsunami. Feel your face turn pink as it burns (but take care not to catch sight of your blotchy cheeks in a shiny surface) and your fingertips tingle. Now feel the warm film of sweat coat your skin from top to toe and picture a bead or two trickle down your sides…

Don't fret, it'll only last a few minutes, but I guarantee that, like the Spanish Inquisition, it'll take you by surprise (no one expects the Spanish Inquisition). You'll probably be in the middle of giving a presentation at work, or flirting with someone half your age. And it could return at at any time, maybe only a few minutes later.

What to do? Well, you could ignore it and blunder on, even though your brain feels as if it's cooking, or you could find somewhere where you can sit very still until it passes. A glass of cold water is more useful than a glass of wine, and more palatable than some of the foul-tasting natural "remedies" on offer.

You could see your doctor and get yourself pumped full of synthetic chemicals, but that seems a bit extreme and, so I'm told, only puts things on hold. Or you could do what I do – turn to your loved one and, completely out of the blue, give him an earful. It doesn't matter what about, just let rip like a deranged lunatic. It won't help, but then I never said I had the answer...

I have to go now and take a cool shower – tonight is not a good night. So, guys, if like my husband you have slunk off to bed with your tail between your legs with a vague feeling that you must have done something really bad (even though you don't remember it), take heart. It's probably not your fault. That said, it's not her's either. Next time, get a nice cool drink and ride it out. And if you value your testicles, pour one for her too.

2018 Note: *Interesting aside - this was the blog post that received the most hits, apparently due to its deliciously google-able title. A complete and innocent accident on my part, I assure you - how was I to know it would appear when "Hot over 50s" was typed into a search engine? Still makes me chuckle when I imagine the disappointment some searchers would have felt when they landed on it...*

LETTER TO MY BROKEN HEARTED DAUGHTER

Dear B,

It's been over a month now since you left your hometown. You've been away before – to Uni for a year at 18, backpacking alone across the US at 19 – but I'd kind of got used to having you nearby. I guess most parents would have thrown up their hands in horror when their daughter announced she was jacking in her job and taking off to work a summer season by the sea, but my parenting has always had at its core a policy of benign neglect. Besides, your dad and me, we knew it was time for you to fly away again.

You didn't reckon on having to deal with a broken heart and I didn't reckon on not being able to give you a hug when you needed it. I'm so glad you've made such good friends, as you do wherever you go, but I wish I could spend even an hour face to face so that I can see for myself you're all right. The need to touch you, to be in your physical presence is a powerful, visceral force that takes my breath away.

I remember the bitter, metallic taste of a broken heart: that pounding, sinking, sickening feeling, that salty rage that breaks over you in waves and makes your heartbeat throb in your ears, that red-tinged madness that feels as if it will never, ever end, leaving you hollow and empty.

But it does end, my darling girl. It will ebb and flow and, eventually, quieten to gentle sorrow and even, hard though it might be to believe just now, a gratitude for the good times you had. My advice, if only I was near enough to give it, is to allow yourself to feel every emotion that pummels you. Ride them out, don't push them away or they'll be back to bite you on the bum when you least expect it. So be sad, be mad, then move on.

You'll recognise love when it finds you again, and you'll never accept anything but the kind that cherishes and nurtures you in equal measure to the love you give. Don't allow yourself to hide your heart away for too long – protect it, but don't steel-coat it. Love yourself first and foremost, for you are the most loveable woman, the most deserving soul. (Start with loving your liver …!)

Believe me when I tell you, you will survive: so long as you know how to love, I know you'll stay alive. For you've got all your life to live and you've got all your love to give and you'll survive, you will survive, hey hey!

Now I've come over all derivative, I know it's time for me to sign off. You probably won't even read this, or at least not for a while, but I feel better for having written it. I'll see you next month but, meanwhile, you know where I am when you need me. And if you don't, well, that's okay too. I love you, child of my heart, and wherever you are, sober or otherwise, I hold you close to me.

All my love, always,

Mum xxx

WHAT ARE *YOU* DOING ABOUT IT?

Whenever I went to my dad with a gripe about how unfair things were, he would always reply: *"What are YOU doing about it?"* It didn't matter what it was, how big or small the problem, that was his default answer and it drove me crazy.

Of course, when I had children I developed a variant of my own: *"It's not what happens to you in life that counts: it's how you deal with it."* As I've got older and witnessed how different people deal with different things my belief in that saying has solidified – attitude is everything.

What we give out is what we get back. The subconscious mind doesn't know the difference between reality and what we tell ourselves. So if it hears us saying *"nothing good ever happens to me,"* it hangs on to that belief so tightly that even when the good stuff comes along, there's a part of us expecting it to end. Which it will, since nothing, good or bad, lasts forever, and that negativity is then reinforced.

We all get locked into negative spirals at some points in our lives, and breaking free seems far from easy. But when we consider that life happens in the present moment, we know that change is possible in a heartbeat.

If you're feeling despair right now about whatever issue, I send you my love. More importantly, I hope that you will feel moved to take the time to think about what is distressing you and ask yourself: what am *I* doing about it?

LETTER TO MY HUSBAND

Hi, Hon.

Today marks the beginning of our 30th year of marriage – how did that happen?

Can it really be more than 30 years since you approached me bravely in Genevieve's (Students and Nurses night)?

I was 18, you were 21. I had a waist and you had hair. And I knew, the moment you hove into view that you were THE ONE. How? Well, I was so drunk that all I could see was the nebula of light around your blond hair that lit you up like an angel. That and the fact that you didn't run a mile when I asked you to walk me to the ladies (I was too scared I'd fall flat on my face if I tottered off on my own).

The next morning, I woke up to find an unfamiliar ring on my finger – your silver threepence, remember? – and it all came flooding back. When you came to claim your ring back, you saw the contents of my fridge (sausages and Guinness) and you took me back to yours to feed me. From that Shepherd's Pie on, I was hooked and you've been cooking for me ever since. You lucky, lucky man!

Marriage sometimes gets a bad rap these days. Even now, I can't bring myself to be PC and refer to you as my "partner" – you are my husband, not someone with whom I play Bridge or earn a living.

We're not "smug marrieds", we've had our ups and our downs, but somehow we've made it through so far, sometimes through sheer stubbornness. Like the time I told you I wanted to try living on my own for a while and you responded: "Don't be so bloody ridiculous – what do you want for your dinner?" and I, having thought long and hard about my "decision", was so taken aback, replied, "fish?" Well, I was hungry. So, thank you for that. In the last resort there's always dinner.

There's a lot to be said for a shared life. We've made a family together, creating a circle of love that is ever-expanding, always ready to make room for more as the family grows. And we have grown, together.

Thank you for the space you give me, for the love that, whilst it sometimes whispers in the background rather than sings aloud is, I know, always there. I don't need diamonds and flowers to know that you love me.

Scratch that: I don't need flowers.

GOODBYE TO THE BUS

For various reasons I have been travelling by public transport this past 18 months. Maggie Thatcher famously said *"a man who, beyond the age of 26, finds himself on a bus can count himself as a failure"*. Hm. No comment.

My father's pride never allowed him to set foot in one: he would walk miles rather than be seen waiting at a bus stop.

Actually, I wasn't so fussed. I missed my car mainly for the freedom it represented but my new job was accessible by bus and I was too busy to do anything much outside work. It was trickier once I started my business, though: appropriating my husband's car regularly hasn't been ideal for either of us. Nor has standing at the bus stop through the freezing winter, or sweltering through the summer because the bus company never turned the heating off in the buses.

So today is a Red Letter day for I have at last been able to buy another car. I am ecstatic, and yet, and yet...

I shall miss the collegiate atmosphere of the bus in the mornings as the same familiar faces yawn and nod sleepy acknowledgements. I shall miss the drivers I have come to know, especially Mick who always dropped me between two bus stops, at the end of my road, because he said I looked tired at the end of the day.

I shall miss the glorious countryside views that I could stare at instead of having to concentrate on the road ahead. And the feeling that I'm doing my bit for the environment by using public transport.

But I shall embrace my reclaimed freedom and I'll never take having a car for granted again.

THE ULTIMATE IN
COUCH POTATO CHIC

Since I'm on holiday, I've had the chance to take a leisurely look through the papers, even the plethora of supplements that normally go straight into the recycling bin. I picked up *Telegraph Select: Lifestyle Solutions* for readers of the *Daily Telegraph*, preparing to have a chuckle at the bamboo bead car seat covers, the mat that you can roll up to keep your jigsaw puzzle intact and other equally superfluous gadgets that I never knew I wanted.

Imagine my surprise, my horror, my dismay when I found I was still looking at it half an hour later! My eye had been taken by the Snuggle-soft fleece blanket with large, loose sleeves and foot pockets described thus:

"The snuggle blanket is a gigantic fleece blanket with large, loose sleeves and foot-cosy pockets, Designed to keep your entire body wrapped-up and cosy, hands remain free to talk on the phone, eat, click TV remotes, read a book, type on a laptop or even knit (!) Feet cosy in 30cm deep foot-pockets ensuring the blanket moves as you do, keeping the furthest extremities from chilly draughts. For use indoors or out, this new delight replaces any throw or multi-purpose blanket. Made of soft, 210g/m2, non-pilling, 100% polyester fleece. It's machine washable and measures W140 x L190cm."

I love the pseudo-technical information at the end! Plus the proud boast that it's made of 100% polyester. The accompanying photograph shows an attractive young woman on a sofa in a modern – ie: presumably centrally-heated home – lounging on a sofa. This model doesn't appear to have the handy pouches to hold the TV remote and a snack as other I have seen, but it does incorporate the innovative foot pockets, that allow you to shuffle from couch to fridge and back again, so you could always time your snack run with the need to switch channels.

I wonder why the model appears to be so slender? After all, she obviously doesn't need to move around sufficiently to generate her own body heat, not now she's the proud owner of a snuggle-soft fleece blanket. Winter is almost upon us – pass me my cheque-book!

You too can can buy online. Search for "snuggle blanket". And, oh my goodness! Be still my pounding heart - there's currently a buy one get one free offer!

INFANT ESPIONAGE AND DISGRUNTLED HUSBANDS

As the kids return to school this week, my grandson has informed me proudly that he is about to start "Deception". The mind boggles. They seek him here, they seek him there, they seek my grandson everywhere...

Isn't it wonderful when we are honoured with a glimpse into the mind of a child? Like an unsolicited smile from a baby, a conversation with a four year old is a precious thing, something to be treasured.

I was never brilliant at the practical side of parenthood – "Jo's routine" is a true, pure oxymoron – but I loved reading and talking with them. With my grandchildren there's no requirement for me to see to it that they are fed or disciplined or have washed behind their ears, I can simply be me and focus on being with them.

I'm guessing my grandson will soon learn how to pronounce his "el" sounds, but I must confess that I will miss hearing him say on the telephone that he "ruvs me rots."

Husband of my heart doesn't love me very much at all today. I've spent the Bank Holiday weekend digitally processing photographs, catching up with my paperwork and working on this blog. Meanwhile he, apparently, has been gardening, including wading into the pond to mend a broken pump. He tells me over dinner that it was cold and things bit him and he almost fell over. He's sulking because I wouldn't have noticed him floating face down until I started to feel hungry and went to see why he wasn't cooking dinner. Sadly, I think he's right. Oh well, never mind.

WANTED: YOUNG, COOL AND TALENTED PHOTOGRAPHER...

That was the ad I read this morning. Wow, thought I – one out of three ain't bad: where do I sign up?

Turns out that this is an ad to join two brothers: Walter and Patrick Hessert on their year-long road trip around America in their airstream bus. The Million Dollar Road Trip (MDRT) is a venture, funded by selling advertising space on the side of the bus, which aims to "inspire young people to dare to dream and do, to think and act boldly. Now."

Hmm. 12 months in a bus with a couple of guys selling advertising space and awarding "inspiration grants" to young people (under 35) who are following in the great American spirit of entrepreneurialism probably isn't for me, no matter how young, cool and talented I might be.

It's made me think, though: how about a British equivalent?

Wanted: middle-aged, cranky and creaky-jointed photographers for caravan trip around the British Isles. Grants awarded for anyone over 50 who can moan endlessly about the weather whilst simultaneously blaming the government. Must like tea.

Would it take a year? Could we, like the MDRT, plan our route according to the "festivals and marquee events" planned throughout the year? I think we could, y'know.

Seriously – how great would it be to travel around documenting British life through the public events that bring us all together? From the Edinburgh Tattoo to Glastonbury, from the WI tent at local county shows to countless village fetes…I feel a project coming on.

Anyone like to join me? Or sponsor my bus?

2018 Note: *I loved some of the responses this blog post provoked: Regular commentator from the US, "Old Fool" wrote: "Can I bring wine? Can I wear a kilt? Will there be frequent pee stops? Do I have to get up early? Will moderate grumpy be tolerated? How many people in how small a space? I'm probably not a candidate anyway as it would take a long time to get there since I no longer fly but it sounds like great fun." while the very British "mummystime" asked: "Where do I apply??? I can make great tea as well, and the odd cake…"]*

FEEL THE FEAR

Given that the sub-conscious mind, rather like an iceberg, is rumoured to comprise 90% of the psyche, it seems sensible to incorporate ritual and symbolism into life on occasion. Merely saying that you feel calm, or confident is one thing, performing some kind of ritual such as counting to ten before you lose your temper, for example, is another.

Six months ago I made a conscious decision to seek change in my life. I'd had one of those periods we all experience in life that had left me feeling tired and worn down and, on occasion, clinically depressed. How to change?

There are certain things over which we have no control. The only power we have is to choose how to react. Sometimes we are too tired and battered to recognise that we have any power left, but as the queen of affirmations, Louise Hay, famously said, "the power is in the present moment," and I happen to believe in that as solidly as others might hold religious belief. Effective change can only ever come from within.

So I sat down and thought about what I perceived to be the cause of my discontent, what I wanted to do with the rest of my life and what was holding me back. I wrote out a list of negative emotions, such as "guilt", "fear", "self-doubt" and a list of positive feelings such as "confidence" and "self-belief".

I then invited some girlfriends for supper and a couple of bottles of wine and set up a "Bonfire of the Vanities". We each picked blind three "negative" words and three "positive" from a bag, then burned the negative in the garden incinerator with positive intent. (The last is important – you have to really mean it!)

It was only a bit of fun, but it was truly cathartic. Imagine my horror, then, when I checked the incinerator the following morning, and what do you think I found staring back at me? A pile of ash with "self-doubt", barely singed, sitting on the top. WTF? I can tell you that I experienced an icy thrill of horror pass through me, swiftly followed by pure rage. Running for the matches, I proceeded to make sure that sucker burned to dust!

I thought of my nemesis, self-doubt, this weekend as I prepared to enter my final week of paid employment. It has no room in my psyche now and I'm keeping the metaphorical matches at the ready. Nevertheless, I know it's lurking…

LETTER TO MY SON'S NEW GIRLFRIEND

...Just kidding! Would I really do that to you?
Looking forward to meeting her though...

WHO WOULD HAVE THOUGHT IT?

...me, a photographer?

Life has a way of surprising us at times and it certainly has surprised me this year! Twelve months ago I was flat broke and 12 weeks into a new job that was making me miserable. My last child had left home and my husband's business was negotiating turbulent times. I felt ill, exhausted and depressed. There didn't seem to be much to look forward to and I felt as if I constantly had a cloud of negativity swirling around my head.

If there's one thing about depression, it's boring. I was sick of thinking about myself and how I felt, sick of not wanting to get up in the morning and sick of being trapped inside my own head. So sick, in fact, that I decided to undertake an experiment. Believing, as I do, in the laws of attraction, I set out to make a change in my life. What did I have to lose?

We all need to conduct a personal audit every now and then. Personal relationships aside, my achievements included studying for my degree (in International Studies) with the Open University and going on to gain my MA in International Relations in 2007.

For thirty years I have been a facilitator: a support system for my husband and four children. Don't misunderstand, that was my choice and I was happy to have been there for them. But it meant that somehow, over the years, I lost sight of me.

Sound familiar? Taking a long, hard look at myself, I realised that I no longer felt comfortable being visible: even my books and articles were published under a variety of pseudonyms!

That is why my name is on this blog and on my business. This is my way of announcing: "Here I am – this is me and I have something to say." It doesn't matter whether you agree with me, or like what I do. I know I have a right to be here. It doesn't matter that I'm approaching 50 and my hair is greying – I will be seen and heard.

I honestly don't know what I was afraid of before, I only know that I'm not prepared to live the rest of my life fearfully. It's time for me to nurture myself the way I have nurtured my family. Time for me to explore my potential and become the person I've always felt I could be.

So today is important for me: today is where the next chapter begins. Deciding to make something happen was the first step in "things" happening! Since starting the blog I have met so many positive, life-affirming people and that has rekindled my own positivity. Although I lose confidence every now and again, I haven't allowed myself to lose focus. I've forged ahead with setting up my photography business and writing the blog and things seem to have fallen almost effortlessly into place. Suddenly, everything I'm doing feels right. I don't over-think it, I just go with the flow.

So stick with me, folks – together we can soar beyond the limitations we impose on ourselves. For I am fabulous – and so, I suspect, are YOU!

50 WAYS TO FLOURISH AT 50
Numbers 6-10

Look after your mental health. Seek help for persistent mental pain in the same way you would seek help for the physical.

Don't waste energy trying to appear younger than you are. You're not kidding anybody, and besides, there's nothing wrong with being - and looking - as if you're 50 years old. Embrace the "characterful" features life has given you. You don't have to slash, burn and poison yourself into being "good enough". Know that you are beautiful, just as you are.

Conversely, good grooming and maintaining an interest in fashion has the power to lift the spirit.

Hair growing in unexpected places is a new fact of life. Epilate, or learn to live with it. Do the latter, and learn to live with horrified glances in public places too.

Moisturiser is now almost as essential as air. Face and body both look and feel better with supple skin

REALITY TV IS NO LONGER FOR ME

I have a confession to make. I like watching TV programmes where people win life-changing amounts of money, or have a hidden talent discovered or lose a stone a week through extreme exercise. It cheers me up, cheering them on. Or at least, it did.

Son no. 2 – the musician – has nagged me for years not to watch shows like the "X-Factor" a) because they've "ruined" popular music by sanitising the music and manufacturing the acts, and b) because they are rigged. He has a friend who is a contestant on the current season and he tells me she is "scheduled" to go out in the semi-finals.

So far, I have turned a deaf ear to all his pleas, choosing to believe that, on these programmes, dreams really do come true – because I want to believe it. I still believe in fairytales, Santa Claus and Disneyland magic.

The X factor franchise, owned by Simon Cowell's SYCOtv, began in 2004 when it replaced "Pop Idol". We Brits have always loved talent shows – who can recall Hughie Green and "Opportunity Knocks", or "New Faces"? The X factor, however, along with "Britain's Got Talent", "Britain's Next Top Model" etc are a whole new ball game.

Last night, I watched the desperate guy with the decent voice for whom the show is a last chance perform. The producers had clearly decided to play up the desperation and styled him accordingly, thus setting him up for ridicule. I watched the camp duo in sparkly pink and lilac suits strip down to lycra cycling shorts and prance about, inviting us to laugh at the gay people. Then there was the fragile girl with the on-trend voice who got through despite dramatising a sore throat and failing to perform at her audition. I listened to the staged bitching between the judges and surfed the wave of frenzied crowd participation who whoop and screech at every opportunity and drown out the performance whenever anyone hits a big note. And I switched it off.

Bored. I'm done. The reason I enjoyed it – for the singing, the fun – has finally been obliterated by the bullying, the deception and the sheer nastiness of the whole event. Some – probably the 13 million plus who watch each episode – might say I'm exaggerating. Some – such as my son – might wonder what's taken me so long.

So long "reality TV", hello reality. From now on I'm going to read a book on Saturday nights.

2018 Note: *I have to say that, since I wrote this blog post, there seems to have been a softening in some - though by no means all - of these programmes. Maybe I wasn't alone in my opinion.]*

PARTY ON!

Preparations are afoot for my 50th birthday celebrations. I've never had a birthday party, not as an adult anyhow. To be honest, the thought both thrills and horrifies me by turns. What if no one comes? Why wouldn't they? I don't know! I can't legislate for my neuroses. It feels a bit show-offy, making myself the centre of attention, but on the other hand, for once in my life I want to mark a personal milestone with a public statement.

My daughters have kindly taken on the organisation, which is why it's being discussed so early – who knows where in the world daughter no.2 will be in a month's time? We're thinking   village hall, band, fish and chip supper and a rockabilly theme. That might change yet, of course. I might yet get cold feet and decide to spend the big day with the duvet over my head.

THE TRACKS OF MY YEARS

Whenever I hear the Platters singing "Great Pretender" I think of my dad. He would sing it badly, but with real feeling, and I knew it had a significance for him. I also think of him whenever I hear Johnny Cash. We were going to play one of his favourites: "Ring of Fire" at his funeral, but since it was a cremation we held back.

Now I find that certain songs remind me of my children. Music played on long car journeys, and mix tapes made by each of them of their favourites. Songs Son no. 2 chose to play (*ad nauseum*) when he was learning guitar. Tunes that daughter no 2 would dance to around the living room. They make me feel wistful, but also envelop me in a big fluffy blanket of happy memories.

I'm useless at remembering song titles and who sang what, so I sent out a text to the four of them asking them to tell me what they feel sums each of them up. It provoked quite a debate. I was reminded that "Daniel" by Elton John was bastardised for son no. 2, the youngest's benefit to "Daniel my brother, you are younger than me, do you still feel the pain? – doosh!" and someone would whack him.

I remember them singing along to Sugar Ray "Every morning" on holiday in Florida, dozing to early REM in the back of the car on the way home from Wales. Their dad playing "air sax" to Gerry Rafferty's "Baker St" while I yelled at him to keep his hands on the wheel (he'd lick the imaginary reed first too). Spin Doctors "Two Princes", Dire Straits "Sultans of Swing", the Beatles and

Radiohead. Greenday's

"Nice Guys Finish Last", was picked my Son no.1's so-called mates as the song that represented him when he was at school. Happily, he remains to this day, a nice guy, though not financially wealthy, it has to be said. Mind you, that was an improvement on "Let's all go to Tesco's where Blackwell gets his best clothes: his shoes are really nifty, they're only one pound fifty…"

"Millenium" by Robbie Williams and "Mr Mistoffelees" from Cats – they were an eclectic bunch. Offspring, "Really Fly for a White Guy" and Status Quo – *I like it, I like it I lullula-like it here we go -oh! Rocking all over the world!* Bowie, TRex, Steve Harley, Wings, Madness…

"Eternal Flame" by the Bangles, "Tell me on a Sunday" by Elaine Paige and Queen: always Queen. Bohemian Rhapsody in four part disharmony, *"I want to break free-eeee"*. Slapping their thighs and clapping in time to "we Will Rock You," and screeching along to the soaring "Barcelona". Happy (if noisy!) days.

BLAME THE BRAIN!

Louann Brizendine, MD published The Female Brain in 2008. In it, she explains the real difference between the male and female brain: unlike the male brain, a woman's has what she describes as a *"uniquely flexible structure"* that is in a *"constant, dynamic state of change"*. Oo-er - does that ring any bells with you?

Which of us doesn't know of at least one menopausal woman who suddenly steps outside the familiarity of hearth and home and starts again - alone? Maybe you are that woman, either practically or metaphorically?

Personally, my experience is of the latter - part of my purpose in starting to write this blog was to satisfy an urge to re-establish myself as an individual in my own right after years of (quite happily) nurturing others.

According to Brizendine, this often shocking development can be attributed not just to psychology, but to a measurable biological reaction in the mature female brain. The ebb and flow of hormones through a woman's menstrual cycle are designed to ignite her nurturing impulses, to tune her in to every nuance of emotion of other and are designed to flood the brain with oxytocin and dopamine, the feel-good hormones that reward her for performing her caring role.

Once the rocky years leading up to menopause are over, however, there is more constancy in the flow of impulses through her brain. The result? The mature woman's brain becomes more like a man's.

"Starting at about age 43, the female brain becomes less

sensitive to oestrogen, touching off a cascade of symptoms that can vary from month to month and year to year, ranging from hot flashes and joint pain to anxiety and depression...The level of oestrogen drops as does that of testosterone - the rocket fuel for sex drive. The 24 months before menopause... can be a rocky ride for some women."

You think? Why does no one tell us this stuff? Doctors seem to simply write prescriptions for anti-depressants and without explanation. Maybe if we knew we were likely to feel like adolescent girls (without the fun, as Brizendine puts it) at least we wouldn't feel as if we were going mad. Incidentally, the brain also has been shown to have a dramatically altered response to glucose at this time, causing cravings for sugar and carbs. So even greed can be blamed on hormones!

During the menopause, we start to "unplug" our "mummy brains" and often look for personal fulfilment beyond our families. Brizendine warns that for those of us in long relationships it is important to question whether hormones play a part in any discontent we might feel - blaming our partners and leaving home is often akin to throwing the baby out with the bath water. Although men undergo hormonal changes of their own, they do not experience the sudden, dramatic changes that we do and they can be left feeling bewildered. Not half as bewildered as us though, I would suggest!

For what happens when we get our new man-brains? We start to get selfish, that's what, and about bloody time! Once we start to emerge from the hormonal minefield the new, calmer biology in the female brain can be a blessing if we let it be so. The biology of the mature brain helps us to let our children go and, at the same time, turn our attention to other interests. Now is the perfect time to learn something new, change career and generally reassess what we want from the rest of our lives.

And if you want to *understand* what's happening to your neural pathways, read this book. You too, guys - it might actually give you an insight into the way women think, or at least explain why they appear (?!) to be erratic.

LETTER TO MY FATHER

Hi Dad, it's me, Jo.

Hard to believe it's been 15 years since I held your hand, 15 years since I kissed your familiar, *Old Spice* scented cheek.

I wish you'd allowed us to talk about the fact that you were dying. We all had to say goodbye in so many coded, oblique ways in those seven short weeks of your illness. Do you remember? I said to you, "I can't imagine a world without you in it," and that was the closest you allowed me to come to "I love you."

The nearest you came to admitting you knew you wouldn't be leaving the hospice was: "do what needs to be done." You meant, *don't let me suffer* and the wonderful staff there made sure that you didn't.

It's true that time is a great healer. After 15 years I don't think about you every single day. There's a dull ache in my heart instead of the take-your-breath-away pain of recent loss. The words *I'm sorry* no longer whisper endlessly inside my head. There'll always be a you-shaped hole at the dinner table at Christmas and other big family events, but life has gone on, as it has to.

I wonder what you would have made of life in the 21st century? I remember you shouting into one of the first mobile phones at the checkout in Tesco's and feeling absolutely mortified. Would you have embraced all the gadgets and technology we have now?

Mortification was a feeling you invoked in me on many an occasion through my teens. Such as when you wrestled me to the ground and tickled me until I cried in front of a new boyfriend. Or when you insisted on mixing up your words so that anaglypta wallpaper was always "eucalyptus" and the accelerator (gas) pedal in the car was the "exhilarator". You always had a chip on your shoulder the size of the Oxford Dictionary about your lack of education, and yet you were one of the most intelligent and knowledgeable people I have ever known.

When I was a child you were always so smart, so handsome. I can see you now, using a match to burn the shoe polish into the leather of your shoes, even polishing the strip of leather   underneath between heel and sole. I always loved to see you in a suit and tie.

I remember your 50th birthday party, how happy you were, how bashful that so many had turned out to celebrate with you. For years after you died, I couldn't remember all the happy things, I only remembered the last five years. After Mum left it was as if you gave up. You didn't want to move on with your life and once all your energy had been spent in the fruitless campaign to win her back, you turned inward and, ultimately, neglected yourself to the point of expiry.

There's a saying in Native American culture that elderly people, when they know their time is near, "turn their face to the wall" and I honestly believe that's what you did. Only you weren't elderly, Dad, you were 58. *Fifty eight*. You never got the chance to be elderly.

I was angry with you for a long time for that – for giving up at 53. For not feeling that your family was enough. You were the fulcrum of the wheel that was our family and, once you were gone, we all went spinning off in different directions, so there was even more than you to miss.

When my mother died you were only 24 years old – self-destruction wasn't as easy then, though by all accounts, you had a good try. Meeting and marrying mum was your renewal, your second chance. You worked so hard for us, both of you did. Family was everything to you.

You were a cantankerous old bugger, of course. What I would give to be able to argue with you again! We'd have fallen out over so many things and you'd have interfered with the way I raised my children, who loved you so much. Did you see how badly they were affected by losing you?

For a long time, your grandchildren thought that the North Star was you, watching over them. You followed them wherever they went and the thought comforted them. One of them has a small star tattooed on her inner wrist for each person she has loved and lost. Yours is the largest, the dominant one. You'd hate the tattoo, but love the sentiment.

You never recognised how much you were loved, or how many friends you had. Why was that? *A friend is only an enemy you don't yet know*, you'd tell me. Who let you down so badly that that thought, that mangling of the saying *"a stranger is just a friend you don't yet know"* was so ingrained?

How could you not have known how well-loved you were? I turned around at one point at your funeral and was shocked to see how many men had packed into the crematorium and how much raw emotion trembled in the air between them.

For all your insecurities, you were one of life's energisers. You were a giver, the life and soul, the patriarch. The love we all had and have for you is testament to the kind of man you were.

I would know this anniversary is approaching without recourse to a calendar because the air becomes clear and crisp and there's the faint scent of bonfires in the breeze. That night, I left the hospice for the last time to a perfect, cloudless, navy blue sky and the scent of pine needles and bonfires. It was still and quiet, oddly so. I knew that nothing would ever be the same again, that this was the reality of a world without you in it. We would all have to get used to a new kind of normal.

Today your children will acknowledge you, each in our

own way. For me, this year, I have written you a letter. I wrote it for you, but also for me and for anyone reading it who has lost a much-loved parent. It's a pitiful letter in that I just can't seem to get it right, to find the words to express what I want to say. Some things will always be locked in my heart. So I will just say this:

I love you. I miss you and I am so grateful to have had you in my life for the time that we had. I have always been so proud to be your daughter.

With love, always, Jo

2018 Note: *This post provoked a response from members of my family who had never in fifteen years spoken of the traumas we had shared over the five years of our father's decline, opening channels of communication and healing for which I will always be grateful.]*

MY FOOT AND MY MOUTH ARE WELL ACQUAINTED…

…because "putting my foot in my mouth" is a regular habit of mine. I'm telling you this because, if we meet in the "real" world and you are the easily offended type, I guarantee that I will offend you, probably early on in our acquaintance, and I wanted to warn you in advance. I don't mean it, it's just that my brain and my mouth don't always connect as quickly as I'd like them to, and I have a "certain way with words". The kids call them "mumisms".

Let me give you an example. Recently, I went for dinner at the house of a new friend and her husband, a complete stranger to me. I took two bottles of wine: a Chardonnay and something red, and when asked, said I'd like the white, please. On tasting, I found the wine was sharp and fruity and, embarrassed that I'd bought crap wine, apologised. "I'm really sorry – the wine is awful!" Of course, it wasn't my wine I was drinking, but a Sauvignon my hostess had open in the fridge.

Luckily, in this instance, my insultee was on my sense of humour wave length and saw the funny side. And in my defence, if it *had* been a Chardonnay, it would have been dire, but you can see my problem.

I once told Daughter No. 2 that I'd bought her a watch that I thought suited her because it was plain. I meant that it was a practical choice because it would match any outfit, but it took some explaining.

The first time I met my eldest daughter's partner, I

wanted to ask him where his name (Frank) came from –
was it a family name, or short for Francis, was what I
thought I said, but it actually came out as: "so…is there a
reason you're called Frank?" (I then proceeded to down a
glass of water so fast that it started to pour out of my nose
and I had to go and be sick in the kitchen sink, but that's a
drinking problem).

Husband of my heart (BSc. C.Eng. M.I.C.E.
M.I.Struct.E) once commented that he felt that he and son
no. 2 were the runts of the litter when it came to intellect
in our family. To which I replied: "I think Daniel's quite
clever, actually."

Anyway, I hope now that if you meet me, you'll be
prepared. It's fairly likely I'll say something peculiar. At
least now you know that I don't mean any offence. So
please try not to take any!

ALONE, AT LAST

Earlier this evening, I checked in to an anonymous motel at a motorway service station. Calm down at the back there – this is not that kind of a story! I'm on a course for the next couple of days and, to be honest, I wasn't looking forward to the long drive down here on a Sunday evening. But you know what? As soon as I walked in, I could feel myself relax.

Most people abhor cheap chain motels. They are anonymous, homogenous, lacking in character. Yep. And that is why I love 'em!

I booked with confidence, knowing exactly what I was getting: comfortable bed, desk and chair, sofa, coffee table, TV, the kind of art on the walls your eyes skim over (ok, I concede that last bit's not so good). There's everything I need in the bathroom, somewhere to hang my coat, spare blankets, a hairdryer and a kettle. It's clean (and if it wasn't, I'm confident it would be put right without a fuss). I've checked out my escape route in case of fire (what? don't you do that?), locked the door and put the chain on, kicked off my shoes and…aaaah. I am completely alone.

I have a confession to make: I like being alone. Not all the time, but regularly – once a day. Sometimes I like to be alone for a day or so. I like my own company and, in my opinion, solitude is seriously underrated. Here, in this anonymous hotel room, there is space for me to be.

I've taken advantage of the free WiFi to prepare for tomorrow and write this blog post. I've eaten the picnic tea I brought with me and made a cuppa with real milk – also brought from home. The Sunday papers await after a hot bath, as does the Free View TV. I will miss snuggling up with Husband of my heart, but it'll come as no surprise to him to hear that I will enjoy sleeping in the middle of the bed!

I can hear the low hum of traffic on the M5 outside, but in this little bubble I feel gloriously, blissfully peaceful. Night night!

ON MOTHERHOOD

This post is for the mothers of adult children – and the men who love them.

If you should ever cut me in half (although I can't imagine any circumstance where you should want to do such a thing!) I swear you will find my children's names running through me, like a stick of rock. It's as if, when they cut the umbilical cord, a million invisible particles were set loose in my bloodstream, infusing me with a part of the soul of the child I had carried. Consequently, they are present in every cell of my body and, for me, this happened four times.

The act of giving birth is so profound. It is like the experience of holding someone's hand as they die: you are changed by it forever. Being a mother is almost a part of the DNA. A little while ago, I wrote about the mature female brain as described by Louann Brizendine, MD. I can relate to her theory that, biologically, when we reach the menopause our brains undergo chemical changes that damp down our protective maternal instincts and allow us to let go. To a point.

You see, you know that feeling we get when our 5 year old stands up on stage to sing in the school play, or our 10 year old takes his first piano exam; as if we are feeling their nerves ourselves? – that never goes away.

Distance is irrelevant: if my daughter is ill, I am willing to travel any distance to make sure she is warm, safe and properly diagnosed. When my son is performing, I want to be there. Break my daughter's heart and, if you see me in the street, I would advise you to duck into a shop for a I swear that I – yes, mild-mannered, crowd-pleasing, law-abiding me – is capable of punching you in the face. And stamping on your man bits as you lie on the ground.

They are adults now, of course, and neither need – nor want – me to fight their battles for them. Plus the last thing they need is to have to worry about me! I know, intellectually, that there is nothing I can do except support and hold my tongue on my advice, unless they ask for it. So how do I learn to be a sieve rather than a sponge?

My anxiety is totally pointless. It's not as if, when they are experiencing difficult, painful things, I can kiss it better and draw a smiley face on a plaster and it will all be ok. My worrying and my love are draining my energy to no purpose. They can't feel it, it doesn't help them. But I feel for them. Uselessly, helplessly, pointlessly feel for them.

So tell me – how does a mother protect herself so that there's something left when practical help is needed?

Answers on a postcard, please

2018 Note: *3 of my 4 children chose to respond to this post. This is what they had to say:*

Son no 1: *"Trust in the fact that you raised your children well. They are all intelligent and strong, capable and fierce when required. Trust that you imbued in them the ability to love completely and hate judiciously. Never underestimate the importance of your being there even if you are not called upon."*

Daughter no 1: *"Listen to Ben."*

Me: *"Bless you both. However, one caveat – I have always taught my children that hate only hurts the hater in the long run. So if those feelings arise, let them be transient. Hateful actions almost always come from a place of fear."*

Daughter no 2: "I agree. but with less big words…Hate is a hard thing to let go of, but you're right you did teach us not to hate and it's a shame that things happen that force that from us, but you did a good job. I for instance didn't punch him in the face I smiled sweetly and was perfectly civil…this comes from you, because my part of the brain was screaming "just hit him". Sometimes it does help to think wwmd (what would mum do) xxxx Also - Treat people as you'd wish to be treated. Karma's only a bitch if you are."

I'M A LITTLE BIT COUNTRY

Whenever I'm feeling vulnerable I reach for country music. It's like bubble gum for the mind – aural comfort. My dad was a Johnny Cash fan; my musician son cut his teeth on the guitar with Cash – the best always endure. So, of course, do the not so good – that's my bubble gum! I make no apology for my love of unsophisticated tunes. It's akin to appreciating steak, but fancying a burger every now and then.

Maybe it was the story-telling element that appealed to me as a kid, maybe it was the simple beats and uncomplicated melodies. I do remember being delighted by such lyrics as *"if I said you had a beautiful body would you hold it against me?"* and *"There's been a load of compromisin' on the road to my horizon..."* that I thought were really clever. I was always a bit of a wordsmith.

In Country-world, the guys had a better time of it than the gals. They were expected to Stand by their Man even though: *"you'll have bad times while he has glad times, doin' things that you don't understand..."* and you'll have to beg unscrupulous harlots like Jolene not to "take" your man just because she can. And what about that poor girl who's been told it's over 10 times, despite the fact that Faron Young *"saw more love in her eyes when I left her than most foolish men will ever see"*? Dawn "woke up the wanting" in him – ahem – and now for the tenth time he's changing his mind. Even as a youngster I remember thinking: I hope she tells him where to get off!

LETTER TO MY SONS

Hey, boys – did you think you'd got away with it when I wrote my letter to your sisters? hehe – I've been saving this.

Thing is, you were both the sweetest little boys and watching you grow into the men you are today has been a privilege, and one of the greatest pleasures of my life. You've both had your problems as well as your triumphs, but don't worry, I'm not intending to talk about those.

Time was that you used to hang on to my every word, now our time together is so precious, we spend it having fun, not setting the world to rights.

So, where to begin? Not too many words, I guess, or one of you will find his attention wandering and the other will start ending my sentences for me. This, then, is what I want you to know:

- BELIEVE IN YOURSELF. 100%. All the time.

- You don't always have to have all the answers. When a woman tells you she's had a bad day, she doesn't want you to tell her how she can put it right, she just wants you to listen, giver her a cuddle and pour a large glass of wine. If you can manage a foot massage you will probably get lucky.

- However, if she's had a bad day because the washing machine has broken down then she *does* want you to have all the answers. And the right tools to fix it.

- Find time to exercise. The male of the species needs a daily run, much like a puppy, or you'll get fidgety.

- Beer and fags will take their toll. So will whisky.

- Sometimes a toll is worth paying. Just not all the time. Take the scenic route.

- And don't take drugs.

- Pay your bills on time. Save rather than borrow. Spend less than you earn. It's not rocket science.

- Learn to say no occasionally. She'll respect you in the morning. (Just kidding!)

- Stay interested in your career. Find your niche.

- But don't allow yourself to be defined by what you do. It's a cliche, but no one has *"he was a good worker"* engraved on their tombstone.

- Don't forget to shower. And yes, you *do* need. Clean underpants socks and shirt EVERY DAY!

- Wash your bed linen.

- Be aware of your motives. Examine your conscience. Then stick to your guns.

- Love your mum. Be available to help your dad when he needs it, as he inevitably will as he gets older. But aside from that, live YOUR life. Don't look backwards.

- Never forget you are still boys. Kick balls, play computer games, laugh at farts.

- However, don't allow yourselves to be infantilised by computer games, or continue to light your farts - you are men now, not boys.

- Be there for each other, and for your sisters. Friends will come and go, your family will be beside you forever.

That's about it. Nothing you don't already know really, but sometimes it's worth setting these things down. You are, without doubt, two of the best. You both have strong wills and big hearts. One of you, at least, has a reckless streak a mile wide with a smile that matches it, (so that's ok, then).

Keep cheerful, look for the good around you – it is there, if hidden at times. When you are tossed about like matchsticks in the fast flowing river of life, don't forget that there is a safe haven, both in your family home and in my heart. I'll stop there before you drown in cliches.

Keep the faith, boys.

Love Mum xxxx

50 WAYS TO FLOURISH AT 50
Numbers 11-15

In some (usually non-western societies) grey hair will ensure you are treated with respect. It's ok to be grey...or to dye your hair whatever colour you choose. It's your head. Don't let your kids take the place of your father in the disapproval stakes.

Cherish your friends. Now is the time to gather a social network around you so that you are not solely reliant on your partner/children for your social life. If the time comes when you are alone, you'll get by with a little help from your friends.

On friends: never feel you "have enough". New people, new ideas = new energy alongside the old.

Make social media your friend. Online social networks like Facebook, Instagram and Twitter are a means to keep you connected with all generations and can be a godsend if you're ever feeling isolated. Keep yourself safe online by learning how to use the privacy settings properly and have fun. Just don't send me endless invitations to play pointless games, or I'll have to block you!

Seek out the company of children (with their parents' permission, of course!) They will re-introduce you to the concept of wonder. Which is really rather wonderful..

NEW YEAR'S EVE - THE FUTURE HAS ARRIVED!

Of course, not all of us are confident we know where we're going. Some look to the stars for the inspiration and guidance. Here's the exclusive project50 reader's horoscope for this year:

The year ahead looks rosy for those who wear the correct glasses. If you are single, you will find love. If you are in a relationship, you will reach a new understanding with your partner. Mars rising in Galaxy will settle on Snickers in the latter half of the year, meaning that there may be change on the horizon. Embrace it and you will end the year with a new outlook, since you won't be able to see your own feet. Beware men in grey suits making false promises, particularly if you wish to complete your education. The financial aspect of your chart has disappeared over the moon, therefore you would be wise to spend time making love, not money. There might be a new arrival in the latter half of the year which you will find disrupting: this disruption will continue for the next 18 years, so best get used to it. The world will keep on turning, in spite of all our best efforts to burn it, sink it, blow it up and suffocate it. You will find something to enjoy every day if you look for it. Remember to wear the correct glasses.

This Horoscope must be true – it's on the internet.

JO BLOGS

This blogging malarky is a funny thing. Today marks the halfway point of the main project – 6 months. In that time I've met some lovely people, both in "real" life and in cyberspace, I've learned that, sometimes, it's okay to take a break and that I am not superwoman (and if anyone is feeling disillusioned by that statement, you haven't met me!)

I started this blog because I wanted to make something – anything – happen, to shift the stagnating energy in my life around. I didn't anticipate some of the difficult family matters that were to demand my attention – at times the blog has been akin to a howl in the dark - nor, if I'm honest, that my fledgling photography business would grow wings quite as quickly as it has. In 6 months I have been both battered and blessed.

Now that we have entered the year when I will turn 50, I find myself feeling more optimistic about it. That's mainly because I've learned that 50 doesn't have to mean perpetual hot flushes and American Tan tights – unless you want it to! The 50 year olds I have hunted down are new parents and grandparents, winding down careers and starting new ones, running marathons and realising long-held ambitions. Some are simply hanging in there, through the daily grind of work and redundancy, negative equity and decimated pensions.

Life is full of challenges (she says, stating the bleedin'

obvious). Age doesn't change that, but it does alter our ability to cope with them – after all, we've seen it all before. I've been saddened to discover how many of us have suffered with depression and anxiety. There's light at the end of the tunnel if only we are prepared to embrace change.

That seems to be the key – if you can make a friend of change, rather than fear it, there's a lot to look forward to. I'm looking forward to the second half of the project and hope that as many of you as possible will connect and celebrate life with me.

POSITIVITY, PLEASE

*"The mind is its own place, and in it self
Can make a Heaven of Hell, a Hell of Heaven."*
~John Milton, Paradise Lost

Hands up who's resolved to give something up this January? Thought so. Here's a thought – if you really feel the need to post a list of New Year's Resolutions on your fridge door, think about changing the language. So, instead of saying you won't eat chocolate, say you'll eat more fruit. Rather than vowing to lose weight, resolve to increase your fitness. Don't tell yourself you'll watch less TV, say you're going to go out more, or read more often.

You get my drift – positive affirmations are so much more powerful than negative statements. The subconscious mind, which is so much larger than the conscious mind, only understands absolutes. If we tell it consistently that we are fat, lazy, lacking in willpower, (or whatever your own personal self-flagellation of choice) it will move to make us feel better by directing us towards the things that comfort us most. In my case, that would be cake and trashy TV. Fail.

Have you ever noticed how negative the English language can be? It was really brought home to me when I spent some time in Japan and found myself the only fluent English speaker in the University program. I hadn't realised how often we say things like: *"Do you not want to go?"* until I was faced with total bafflement. I spent a month checking myself, trying to say *"do you want to go?"* – ie: using positive language – to make myself understood.

We don't realise the drip-drip-drip of gloom that negative thinking causes. *"That's just my luck"*, *"trust me to mess it up"*, *"this country has gone to the dogs"*. *"nothing ever changes"*. Our national Press has a lot to answer for, whipping up moral panics and feeding into national insecurity. So does so-called "reality TV" and soap operas. What do we get out of watching other people being miserable? Does it make us feel better about our own lives? Why do we subject ourselves to it?

Like many people, I'll be dusting down my trainers tomorrow and filling up the fruit bowl. But if there's one resolution that's worth making this year, it has to be to bloody cheer up!

THE ONLY WAY IS UP!

It's official – life begins to pick up at 46!

According to the Economist (average reader age: 47), life is not so much a downward curve into senility from middle age. but rather a "U" bend. That defies gravity, if you ask me, so I read on.

The theory goes that we all start off as pretty cheerful, on the whole, but that this is eroded from youth onwards until we reach rock bottom – the mid-life crisis. Conventional wisdom has it that it's all downhill from there. We lose our looks, our vitality and mental sharpness to varying degrees – what's not to be miserable about?

Well, according to the findings emerging from a study conducted by a new branch of economics, not a bit of it. Once you reach your mid-forties you are on your way to gaining that elusive lifetime goal: happiness.

The new economics measures happiness rather than money as a measure for human well-being. The standard bearer for this measure has been Bhutan where all new policies are assessed for GNH – Gross National Happiness. Then in 2008 top conventional economists, Amyarta Sen and Joseph Stiglitz were directed by French premier, Nicolas Sarkozy, to devise a way of measuring national contentment other than GNP, which measures wealth. Now the British Government have begun to collect data on well-being. Age, of course, is not the only indicator for happiness: personality type, gender, education, marital status, cultural background: all play a part.

Age is one of the more surprising findings. According to the Economist, "People are least happy in their 40s and early 50s. They reach a nadir at a global average of 46."

Conversely, depression peaks at 46. One recent study from Princeton University concludes: "Enjoyment and happiness dip in middle age, then pick up; stress rises during the early 20s, then falls sharply; worry peaks in middle age, and falls sharply thereafter; anger declines throughout life; sadness rises slightly in middle age, and falls thereafter."

Why? The answer, it seems, is down to experience and acceptance. Whilst they experience the same amount of sadness in reaction to distressing situations, older people generally react more philosophically, showing less anger and being less judgemental. They have also generally come to accept their limitations and tailor their ambitions accordingly. Along with life changes, such as no longer being responsible for children, they are generally less stressed than when younger, which also has a positive impact on health.

Of course, none of this is new, but it does bring a positive slant to institutional views of ageing. It will be interesting to see how the Government will utilise its data on GNH. Certainly, it should make them think more roundly about employment and services for the elderly.

For my part, these studies simply confirm what I have long suspected, but so far have only hoped to be true: the gloom that dogged my forties is unlikely to reappear as I move into my fifties. The future might be grey, but it's bright nonetheless!

THE VALUE OF A COMPLIMENT

It sounds obvious, now I come to write it, but praise is a wonderful thing. Allow me to explain: I have entered a profession where I produce and sell something that is easier to sell than anything else I can think of. I sell people their own children. Or pets, or self confidence... As a consequence, I get instant feedback. And praise.

I don't know about you, but I grew up at a time when children weren't particularly praised, for fear of "spoiling" them by making them big-headed. So my inbuilt response to someone praising my work is to redden slightly, maybe even try to point out where it could be improved (I'm such a great business woman!).

Recently, though, I've noticed a change. Perhaps because I've been working so much, and everyone has been pleased with what I've done, I find that I'm less inclined to instantly mitigate compliments and am actually relaxing into it, allowing myself to enjoy the warm glow that a compliment evokes, if only you let it.

I don't think I'm becoming big-headed, (God forbid!) but even I can see that I'm improving all the time. If any of my lovely customers are reading this, then THANK YOU, from the bottom of my heart. Your appreciation of what I do means so much to me, spurs me on to improve and experiment, and has made me very, very happy.

So, who's up for a challenge? It's easy – just find someone to genuinely compliment every day for a week and watch their reaction. I guarantee you'll up the happiness quotient of seven people - eight if you include yourself!

LETTER TO MY YOUNGER SELF

Dear Jo,

If only I could stand at your shoulder and whisper in your ear, there is so much I would like to say to you. If you were still the little girl in the picture I am looking at, I would hold you tight and rock you and tell you that it's ok, YOU are ok, that it's not your fault that some of the adults around you are so screwed up. I would tell you that you are a good, kind girl, that you don't need to be afraid for much longer.

If you were five years old, I'd say, you know that lump in your throat that stops you from swallowing? That's not your fault either. You won't always have to try to beat the clock when you eat so that you can get back to school, that one day, they'll let you have school dinners again, when you learn not to vomit down your tie.

At ten, I would smile at you and let you know that you're not wasting time by reading so much. I'd help you to find the authors you'll grow to love and promise you that even if you were to turn out to be a "blue-stocking", that's ok.

I'd know better than to say too much if I met you at sixteen. I'd only counsel you to take your time: don't be in such a hurry to grow up. This life business, it's not a sprint but a marathon and if you could learn to pace yourself now, you'll save yourself an awful lot of angst later on. But of course, you wouldn't listen. You'd carry on dreaming your secret dreams, about going to Oxford or living in Paris and writing your books and taking lovers that would adore you. but could never touch your heart. And I'd tell you to stay away from Sartre and Nietzsche and for God's sake, to lighten up. Two years ago you had a crush on David Cassidy and read Jackie every week and that was OK.

Of course, now you've discovered sex, and Mum has discovered that you've discovered sex and she's called you names and tried to wallop you, only you've walloped her back and you only compound it by leaving an ashtray under the bed in the bedroom you share with your two sisters. He'll break your heart, you know, but I'm not going to tell you to walk away – he's a lovely boy and it's a lovely time and, despite the aggravation with Mum, you'll never be quite this carefree again.

You don't have to be this scared, you know, at 18 when you arrive at College. I know you don't have anywhere to live, having accepted the place at the last minute, and the only money you have is £15 in a purse round your neck that Dad says is a loan. I wish I could tell you that you're not the only person who feels as if they are looking at life through a film of water that separates them from everyone else. I just wish you could be brave enough to rebel, to really let your hair down, instead of using all that energy on trying to self destruct. I told you that all that Existentialism was a BAD THING.

What would I say to you if I met you at 20? Would I tell you you're too young to walk up the aisle? That you need to learn to be by yourself first? Probably not – this marriage will endure and give you the stability you so clearly need. I'd just tell you to relax – you don't have to hold on so tightly, you can breathe every once in a while. You don't have to be the best mother in the world, just one that cares and does her best. You don't have to be thin, or intense about everything – you'll find your way in your own sweet time.

Most of all, I wish I could tell you in a way that you

would hear: don't waste so much time beating yourself up. It serves no purpose. Stop over thinking everything, give yourself a break. You wouldn't drive the people you love as hard as you drive yourself – save some of that love and care for you. All those years you will lose to depression can never be regained, but don't let that be another stick with which to beat yourself.

You'll be all right, you know. I promise. x

WARNING SIGNS

The blog didn't appear yesterday because I was helping Daughter no 1 and her partner to move out of London to a new town. This entailed a good few hours of driving, a little lifting and carrying (I have my limits!) and a fair amount of tea drinking. Seriously, coming on top of some of my recent travels, I was severely pooped. I considered booking into a local motel before tackling the drive home, but funds were tight and the sofa, surrounded as it was by daughter's life in carrier bags, was not appealing.

I don't drink and drive. Last night, however, I did something that was potentially just as lethal – I drove tired. My eyes were aching half an hour into the journey and it wasn't long before the lights of the cars ahead were shaking. I tried opening the windows, playing music etc, but these manoeuvres had only a temporary effect. The problem with tiredness is that you don't realise that you're falling asleep – until you hit another car, or, as in my case, thankfully, the rumble strips at the side of the road.

We just don't tend to view driving tired as being as dangerous as driving drunk, perhaps seeing it as a matter of stamina rather than irresponsibility. Yet when it comes to drunk driving, once someone has a blood alcohol level over .08, they are considered legally drunk. Studies have shown that a driver who has gone a day without sleep is very similar to a driver with a blood   alcohol level of 0.10%, well above the legal limit. (Source: Sleepdex).   According to the Highways Agency, an estimated 300 people a year die in the UK due to drivers falling asleep at the wheel. They recommend that 15 minute breaks should be taken every two hours when driving long distances, day or night, whether you feel tired or not. A recent report, published in the Journal of Sleep Research, recommends no more than 2 hours driving at night for optimum safety.

All I can say is: thank goodness for those rumble strips. I pulled into the next layby, switched off the engine and rested my eyes for a good fifteen minutes. In future, I will always make sure I have the funds available to book into a motel if I'm too tired to drive. I know I'm lucky to have learned my lesson without hurting myself or others. Today is going to be a duvet day.

"I WISH I WAS A SURFER CHICK..

...with knees that bend and buns of steel, with sun-bleached hair that I could flick, and a life that "keeps it real".

I was back in Newquay, Cornwall last week so that Daughter No. 2 could attend a hospital appointment. It's a 10 hour round trip from home, so we had to stay overnight. Funds are low, so when she suggested we stay in a hostel, I agreed – with some trepidation. I'm nearly 50 for goodness sake: sleeping on a bunk bed in a mixed dorm above a bar isn't something I would normally do. To be honest, I never did it when I was 20 either, so it was always going to be a new experience.

It's low season, so in the event we got a four bed, female only room to ourselves, complete with loo and the tiniest shower I've ever seen. I was propped on a bar stool, plied with soft drinks and treated like a local. I met all her friends, who were lovely, and once I realised that they weren't going to feel awkward that Beth had her mum with her, I decided I wouldn't feel awkward either and relaxed. I even went to Walkabout to the open mic night (and no, I didn't go so far as to embarrass her by getting up to sing!)

I did have to cup my hands round my ears to hear the conversation, and had the p ripped out of me royally, which made me feel at home! I didn't make it past 1.30, but I had a great time. "There's no ageism here, Mum,"

Beth told me as she escorted me back to the hostel. I wanted to tell her that, in my experience, there rarely is in company where tattoos, dreadlocks and guitars feature prominently, but I was pooped. I opened the window so that I could hear the sea, curled up in my remarkably comfortable bunk bed and slept like a teenager.

I don't know how I would have coped with a stranger sleeping on the bunk above me, but there you go. A challenge for another time, maybe? I've always had a secret hankering to travel light and be the kind of person who slots in easily anywhere they go. Someone like my lovely girl, in fact, who fills me with such pride when I see the woman she has become.

It was back to being a responsible mum again in the morning, but it was so good to chill out with my daughter, in her environment, with her friends. It also means I won't worry so much about her when she goes back permanently as I know she has good people around her.

Thanks for making me so welcome, guys. Next time, I'll bring my hearing trumpet.

50 WAYS TO FLOURISH AT 50
Numbers 16-20

The arrival of grandchildren goes a long way towards
compensating for the loss of youth.
Embrace being a Grandma/Pa!

If you haven't "made it" by now in your chosen career,
you probably never will.
Accept where you are.
Or consider a new career...

You're never too old to learn something new. Ergo, you
can still re-train, or study just for the sake of it.

Stop being afraid that you don't know enough. Most
people will assume you know more than you do by virtue
of your age. Just nod sagely, then look it up on your
smartphone later in the loo.

On the other hand, it's probably time to accept that you
don't know everything, and,
you know what? that's ok.

LETTER TO MY BELEAGUERED FAMILY

Dear ones,

Like so many people in these troubled months, we are all having a hard time at the moment. From serious health issues to money worries, joblessness and various emotional crises, we're all feeling a bit battered, whether those things are happening to us, or we're just standing helplessly on the sidelines trying to be a support.

One of you posted on Facebook "Can the universe throw my family a bone already?" Sweetheart, the "bone" we were thrown is to belong to each other. We still find things to smile about and laugh together every time we meet.

It's hard to accept that there are people in the world who seem to sail blithely through life without a thought for the impact their actions have on others, that people you have loved and have loved you can seek to hurt you, but it isn't for us to do Karma's work. It was you who showed me the words of Confucious: "before you embark on a journey of revenge, dig two graves."

Take heed. The best form of revenge is to live life well and be happy.

I am so proud of you all: for your fortitude, your generosity, your stubborn determination to do the right thing, without thought of the cost to your peace of mind. Sometimes, you can't know what "the right thing" is until the years pass and the consequences unfold. You can only resolve to continue to examine your conscience, focus on your goals and not allow yourself to be distracted by the issues and agendas of those who are fighting against you. Conversely, sometimes you have to accept that there is nothing you can do, and move on. Helpless rage never helped anybody.

What I really want to say to you all is, hang in there – this too shall pass. And whilst essentially we are all alone, no man is an island – we will always have each other. Together we stand. Chin up: *Illegitimi non carborundum*. x

KEEP LEARNING

Albert Einstein said: *Education is what remains after one has forgotten what one has learned in school.* Perhaps. "The University of Life" is oft-quoted as their alma mater by entrepreneurs and other successful folk who didn't go through the further education system.

I know for a fact that there are thousands of young graduates in this country working on minimum wage who are left wondering whether they were sold a pup when they were urged to go to university. I know this because two of my children are in this position. The other two, having decided it wasn't worth the debt, dropped out without completing their degrees. Which really makes me sad for them,

You don't need to be in University to continue to learn, but what if you're our age and you've always wished you had completed your degree? Or have a burning curiosity about a subject that requires the intellectual discipline to study in depth to understand it to your satisfaction?

Einstein also said: *Intellectual growth should commence at birth and cease only at death.* I'm with him on that – the day I stop wanting to learn will be the day I give up on life.

I dropped out of college at 19, got married and got on with life, but curtailing my formal   education was always unfinished business for me. I finally achieved my degree (a BA in International Studies) in 2005 after five years of self-directed study with the Open University. The OU is a wonderful organisation, one that, incidentally, is becoming popular with regular students too since they can work and study, thus avoiding running up debt.

Of course, you don't have to study for a degree. The OU has a vast range of FREE (yes, absolutely free) short courses available through the OpenLearn Website where you can satisfy your curiosity about subjects as diverse as mathematics and statistics to an introduction to Art History, Engineering, Climate Change – whatever interests you, you'll find something on the OpenLearn Home Page.

Nervous? I promise you, the OU are experts at guiding you through what's on offer and supporting you once they are studying. Plus their materials are first class. You could spend a lifetime dipping in and out of the subjects that interest you (I know I will!) all without leaving your armchair. And if you DO decide you want to take it further and formalise your learning, there are over 570 courses to choose from at many different levels from short and introductory courses,   certificates and diplomas to undergraduate, postgraduate and research degrees.

Did my degree set me on a path to a new career? No. I went on to study for an MA as a "regular" postgraduate student at an actual University and applied for PhD funding, without success, for three years. Did it change my life? Undoubtedly, in the sense that it gave me confidence, fed my thirst for knowledge and, ultimately, gave me a sense of real achievement.

And how proud was I to be presented with my degree by Betty Boothroyd, (Baroness Boothroyd of Sandwell, to give her her full title), former Speaker of the House of Commons! My family, who had come to see their mother graduate, broke from the tradition of gentle (and genteel) applause to whoop, cheer and yell "go Mum!". "You've brought some support with you, I hear," she said with a twinkle in her eye as she shook my hand.

My forties have been filled with education. I've discovered interesting things, met some wonderful people and had my mind opened to a whole world of different viewpoints, problems and solutions. If that sounds good to you – go for it! It's never too late to expand your mind.

ONCE THE NEST IS EMPTY

We've talked quite a bit about the sadness some of us feel when our nests empty, but it has to be said, if you're partnered, once you get past the shock of facing each other across the breakfast table and realising that yes, you actually have to talk to *each other* unless you want to eat in silence, there are upsides to the children leaving home. Here are a few:

- There's no one around to catch you having a cuddle in the kitchen, ergo, no one will make vomiting noises.

- When you return home after both going out, everything will be exactly as you left it.

- There is food in the fridge.

- And wine/beer

- You don't have to make or buy 7 different kind of cake to cater to all tastes.

- You can play your music without someone shouting *"turn that racket off!"*

- You can sing, if you want to. And dance, without comment being made.

- You can row. This is itself is a seriously undervalued asset. No more hissing-under-the-breath rows that have to go on for days because you keep being interrupted. Now you can slam about and clear the air.

- You no longer have to have silent sex.

In fact, you're free to rediscover all the things you once enjoyed doing together. And, if you're lucky, you might even have the funds to do some of them!

LETTER TO MY MOTHER

Dear Mother,

Today is Mother's Day. I have sent my loving card to the woman who raised me from the age of 4-18, who I am still happy to call "Mum", but I am sending this letter to you. It is a letter I wish could not exist.

They told me that you saw me, just once, before you died, but I suspect that was a kind lie. You had, after all, been rushed by ambulance from Hertfordshire to London after the caesarian. They said that if they hadn't cut me prematurely from you, my life would have been shorter than yours. Below is an excerpt from *your* mother's memoirs, describing those last hours:

...that evening after I left her standing at the gate, I turned at the bend in the road to look back and wave to her. I knew I would not see her again. I don't know how I knew, but the feeling was very strong and I cried all the way home.

A few days later the phone rang at my place of work. It was Roger telling me they were taking Carole to Whittington Hospital in London where there was a neurologist. She couldn't be moved from the Herts and Beds until after the birth, so the baby was being born by caesarian. This was 2nd July 1961. Apparently, there was pressure on the left side of her brain caused by fluid which they had tried unsuccessfully to drain at Bedford. After the baby was born they said she might have a chance if she was kept very still and they could get her to the Whittington. I cannot even imagine the agony of mind Roger must have suffered that day as he lay beside her in the ambulance, trying to hold her still. He told me to wait at home and he would ring me in the evening at my friend's house as soon as he knew anything.

I waited, praying for what, I did not know. My brain felt numb. At about seven o'clock, the doorbell rang. It was Roger. He put his arms around me and said there was very little hope – Carole was dying.

I just wanted to go to the church. Roger fetched Jack and, between them, they walked me to St Mary's. They didn't understand why I wanted this, but they said nothing. I knelt by the altar rail and prayed. Well, God heard my prayers, but he did not grant my request for her life. Hard as it is to understand, I'm sure He knew best.

Carole laid for a week and each day I travelled to North London to see her. She was unconscious, but I felt she knew I was there… The day before she died, on the 13th of July, the doctor told Roger and I that the crisis would come that night. They had no accommodation at the hospital so we were advised to go home.

I lay fully dressed on my bed and, at four am, the police came to tell us she had died.

You were just 21: younger than your granddaughters. I cannot imagine the anguish of carrying a baby to term then not being able to hold it, if you were aware at all. Who would I be if you had raised me? More pertinently, who were you?

That is a question I have asked all my life. It was thought best, as I had never known you, for me to not be told anything at all. Dad promised me that when I was older he would let me have a photograph of you, but that didn't materialise until I was 16.

Even now, I have barely a dozen photographs – enough to know that my smile resembles yours, but I don't know what you looked like when you weren't smiling for the camera, or from behind.

I know, because I have a dress that you made, that you were tiny, though around my height. I know something about you as a child and as a teenager, because Nan wrote about you in her memoirs. I know that you were kind and loving and modest, because that is how your sister remembers you. Dad told me very little. People did what they believed to be for the best. Unfortunately, all my life I have associated my birthday with the tears and mourning of those around me in my early years.

You would be 71 now – probably still very much with us and part of our lives. Of course, then I would not have had mum and my (half) brother and sisters, but putting that aside, I would have loved to have had you in my life, just because you were mine. What would you think of me and my life?

I so wish you could have met your grandchildren, and your great grandchildren. It is through having children of my own that I have been able to experience the mother-daughter bond that I like to imagine we would have had, and I am so grateful for that. I had a connection with *your* mother that I believe can only be attributed to the fact that we were blood. I was her only connection to you, and she mourned your loss to the day she died.

I knew that she loved me, even when years passed without my seeing her. I knew she'd love me no matter what I did, and that certainty was such a crucial anchor for me, and she provided that, partly, for you. It is thanks to her that I have been able to be the mother that I am.

Well, there isn't a lot more I can say. Do I miss you? I never knew you, so I don't know what to miss, but I do know your absence left a hole in my heart that I have never been able to fill. I hope that you would be proud of me, that you would like me as well as love me. I am grateful to you for your fortitude when the pregnancy accelerated whatever it was that killed you, and for the greatest gift of all – my life.

Finally, my biggest regret in my life is that I cannot hold your hand, just once, look into your eyes and speak my heart. What would I say? Simply, that I love you, Mum.

Happy Mother's Day.

Love, Joanna x

ON BLOGGING

I've said this before, but it bears repeating: this blogging business is a peculiar malarky. Did you see that ad for Mother's Day last week? The one where the voice over says: *she's the hands in the picture, the woman with no head in photographs because she's standing behind you, the subject*, etc etc? Well, **project50** started because I wanted to reclaim my space, to become visible again after years of nurturing and supporting others. I decided to raise my head above the parapet, open my heart – however you might like to see it – and move forward unafraid and fully engaged with the world outside my door.

I have to confess, it has been a little scary, at times. I've founded my business, started networking in my local area and created a professional persona, and yet all those people have access to my innermost thoughts, my most inane witterings, even the admission that I do not always feel positive, confident and all those shiny things self employed people are supposed to pretend to be, 24/7.

I've exposed myself, and my family, to public scrutiny, which invites criticism as well as positive connection. I've laid my life bare so that complete strangers, who I have met to interview for the project, know things about me no one usually knows on first meeting. It's weird, in a way, but it also clears the way for me to be absolutely, 100% my authentic self for pretty much 100% of the time. There's no point in feeling insecure, or shy when I walk into a room – everyone there has access to this blog, should they want to read it. They know me, even when I don't know them.

I have yet to decide if this is a good or bad thing. It's good, insofar as most of the feedback is positive, plus it helps when people have heard of you at least when you network with them. However, over the life of the blog, certain events have occurred within my family that have inhibited me, made me censor myself and my output far more than I would like.

I haven't yet, for example, talked about being a grandparent, which is a huge omission in a blog about turning 50. I haven't talked about the impact of children's marriages breaking down, something that many of us are required to process. Certain topics have the potential to upset, anger, or embarrass people I know.

Of course, it is their choice whether they read this blog. It is also their choice to read the factual articles I intend to write over the next few days and see them as a personal polemic. I want to be clear: **project50** was always meant to be a way of connecting with others who are turning 50 and to discuss the important issues that affect us as well as have fun with the lighter articles, photographs and music.

I feel very strongly that I should not allow myself to be censored by worrying about how my words might be taken out of context, or twisted to suit the agenda of others. So if there are topics that matter to you that you would like me to cover, please do get in touch. I would like to create a little more substance to the blog alongside the enjoyable fluff!

2018 Note: *In the event, I never did post those "factual articles" - there was too much at stake to risk retaliation from those who would have misunderstood my motives. Should I have allowed myself to be censored? Sometimes discretion truly is the better part of valour.*

IMAGINE THIS

Human intelligence is a fascinating thing. Right brained, left brained, dyslexic, autistic – the way we think is almost as individual as a fingerprint. "Emotional intelligence" is arguably as valuable to humankind as being good with figures. Creativity is essential to feed the soul. Albert Einstein said:

"Logic will get you from A to B. Imagination will take you everywhere."

Without imagination, the potential of intelligent thought is lost.

Intelligence + Imagination = Application

Or, in the words of the great "imagineer", Walt Disney:

"If we can imagine it, we can do it "

Allow yourself to dream. Imagine the possibilities.

SHE'S LEAVING HOME (*BYE-BYE*)

After a 9 week sojourn at home, daughter no 2 is Cornwall-bound once more. She hasn't had the results of her medical tests yet, and probably won't know anything conclusive for a while, but after a few weeks of rest and tlc she's feeling well enough to start working again. I'm so glad she's ready to return to her life. I'm so sad that, once more, she will be so far away.

I suppose it's inevitable that, with four children, sometimes one or more will fly briefly back to the nest, (usually en route to somewhere more exciting) but it isn't half unsettling for me! It'll take me a few hours to reconfigure the house to how it was before she came back, but it'll take me a while longer to re-adjust to her not being here. I got used to her face being around, and I rather liked it.

Apart from when it was grumpy, which was fairly often, it has to be said. I won't miss the whiff that she brought into the house after she'd been outside for a sneaky fag, or finding she's logged me out of Facebook when my back is turned. I will miss my walking buddy, her kindness and the energy she brought into the house when she was feeling cheerful – which was also fairly often.

Time for me to set aside my selfish thoughts and wave her off once more. She has a   restless spirit that compels her to keep moving on, at least for now, and I would never seek to fence her in. It would be like trying to cage a wild bird.

Take care, my darling girl, and keep this Irish blessing close in your heart:

May the road rise up to meet you, may the wind be ever at your back.
May the sun shine warm upon your face and the rain fall softly on
your fields.
And until we meet again,
May God hold you in the hollow of his hand

WHO AM I?

I met someone the other day who "knows" me through subscribing to the blog. "*You're nothing like I imagined you to be*," she told me (somewhat sadly, I fancy). It got me thinking – who am I? And why is there a disconnect between the "me" who writes on here and the "me" who you see face to face?

As if to underline the point (ie: make me realise that I really do have to address this issue!) my sister remarked that daughter number 2 and I are very alike. Now, anyone who knows her will tell you that no. 2 is bright and feisty, not afraid to say her piece and always up for a boogie. I, on the other hand, am generally quite restrained outside the four walls of my home, sometimes a little nervous and really quite shy. I told my sister this and she said, "I don't mean now – I mean when you were young."

Ouch! She's right. I used to be a much louder, more visible, more vibrant version of the person I am now. So where did she go? Who AM I?

Let me tell you what I think. The "real me" is the person you know on this blog. The person you meet will be a shade of the real me that depends on how much I have allowed myself to be battered by whatever is going on around me. The day I met this lady, for example, I was feeling anxious and tired and was experiencing one of the more tiresome menopausal symptoms – brain fog, so I wasn't as coherent as usual. I can lay my worries aside, of course, when I'm in my professional role. I don't turn up to people's weddings a nervous wreck! But day to day, I allow the vagaries of life to affect me far too much. So if you meet me in "real" life, try not to be too disappointed. I am the person you met here – but I might be a little bit tired and battered!

Enough is enough. I'm nearly fifty, for goodness sake: surely it's time I was my authentic self 100%? I need to practice letting go of the emotional hurly burly that sabotages my peace of mind and live in the moment.

That's going to be my mission in the run up to the big five-oh. Oh, the irony – I am planning to "work hard" at "letting go"! What are the chances of success for that strategy, do you think?

2018 update: *I am happy to say that I no longer recognise my description of myself in this post!*

50 WAYS TO FLOURISH AT 50
Numbers 21-25

Turning 50 is a good time to reflect on where you've been and where you want to go in life. Take some time to work out *your* key needs - whether they be connection to others, financial security, a desire for adventure - and begin to work towards making the things you still dream about a reality.

If you are female, you won't be having any more children. Mourn your lost fertility if you will, but then rejoice.

If you have children, they might be distant physically, but they are still just as precious.
As are you to them. There is still a role for you to play in their lives.

However, take care not to be too closely involved in their day to day lives.
The umbilical cord was cut for a reason
and you will do yourself - and them - no favours if you cling.

We are all different. That's what keeps life interesting. And yet we are all largely the same beneath the surface - take comfort in knowing that you are not alone in your fears and hopes.

LIKE A DOG WITH A BONE…

…I used to worry away at issues large and small. I am one of life's worriers and if I don't keep a grip on the tendency I can drive myself (and those I worry about) insane. Will the weather be fine for the picnic? Will the children get heatstroke? Is the sun block strong enough? It is what it is, I chant silently, like a mantra. *But what if it isn't?*

Funnily enough, it's mainly small, insignificant things that get me these days. The big stuff is easier to rationalise. It used to be that I'd worry about EVERYTHING, from starving children in far flung continents to the man I chatted to at the bus stop who was lonely. And if I wasn't worried, I'd worry that there was something to worry about that I'd missed. It was exhausting

I know I'm not alone. Low level anxiety is a default setting for many. Experiencing anxiety is a normal reaction to stressful situations such as a job interview or being late for a plane. But what if that general feeling of unease, worry and dread persists day in, day out?

According to the NHS, 1 in 20 adults suffer from GAD – General Anxiety Disorder – with it being most prevalent in those in their twenties. That last fact surprises me insofar as it is commonly assumed that it is the middle-aged, particularly women, are most prone to worrying. Perhaps it's just that once we get older we are more likely to be diagnosed with depression or the side effects of hormonal upheavals rather than being saddled with the "GAD" label.

A great deal of worry comes from the need to be in

control, and I gave up on that notion years ago. The tighter you grip the reins of life, the quicker they slip through your fingers.

As for people – trying to control them is a sure fire way to make them run. Unless you break them entirely of course, which is a wholly different kind of tragedy. DH Lawrence documented the ultimate in controlling, passive-aggressive women in his novel, Sons and Lovers. I well remember my gentle-hearted mother-in-law telling me she would never seek to interfere in her child's relationship as she had a fear of *"being a Mrs Morel"*. And she never did, or was.

As for my tendency to worry, I'm a work in progress. It's such a waste of time and energy. Here's "The Nun's Prayer" (author unknown). I am not religious, but this simple mantra resonates with me. This is the first thing I see when I open my eyes in the morning and the last thing I see when I close them at night.

God, grant me the Serenity
to accept those things I cannot change,
the Courage to change the things I can,
and the Wisdom to know the difference

ON HAPPINESS

Did you know that when the New Economics Foundation asked 42,000 people across 22 European countries how happy they were, 8% of British participants said they were bored "most of the time" and 20% said they felt their lives were "neither valuable nor worthwhile."*

UK charity, Action for Happiness, aims to promote "a more co-operative society where people expect more satisfaction from what they give than what they get." Backed by the latest in scientific enquiry, the charity list a series of 10 things you can do to increase your level of happiness:

1.   Do things for others
2.   Connect with people
3.   Take care of your body
4.   Notice the world around you
5.   Keep learning new things
6.   Have goals to look forward to
7.   Find ways to bounce back
8.   Take a positive approach
9.   Be comfortable with who you are
10. Be part of something bigger

One simple, effective strategy to keep the blues away is to develop an attitude of gratitude – taking time daily to reflect on what is good in your life, no matter how small, is the very least you deserve. Write a list. You might find that you're actually happier than you perceive yourself to be after all!

*Reported in the Sunday Times Magazine 3/4/11

ONLINE REVEAL

Some time ago, son no. 2 persuaded me to have a go at an XBox game. It was called Mortal-War-Creed-Assassin or something. It required me to sneak up on people and do unspeakable things to them before they shot me and it was horrible. Not because the graphics were... well, graphic, but because my body started pumping out adrenalin as if it was real.

To be fair, I was the same in 1979 when Space Invaders hit the amusement arcades. Every time one of those pesky little critters got zapped I got more and more stressed because it was MY FAULT! So I have a theory that I thought I'd share with you – I think you can tell an awful lot about a person by their computer game playing style. (Of course, you could argue that you can tell a lot about a person if they play computer games at all, but that's another story).

Take Son No.1. He thinks through his tactics before he even turns the game on – that's a major part of the fun for him. He's a cool-headed strategist, a problem solver – in short, he's a cerebral player. Son No.2, on the other hand, charges in, all guns blazing. While he normally gets cut down within minutes, he takes a heck of a lot characters with him. He's a blunderbuss. When I played with him, he had me screaming "what's your exit strategy?" as he was cut down in a hail of cyber-bullets.

So – one son has a Masters degree in Astrophysics and one is a musician, and no, I'm not running a competition – it's bloomin' obvious which is which, isn't it?

Whereas I am a nervous wreck, especially if I'm coerced into playing computer games!

CONVERSATIONS WITH MY HUSBAND

I love my husband. No, really, I do. But after 30 years of marriage we do get on each other's nerves at times! Take Sunday morning.

Him: My knee hurts.
Me: Oh dear. Why?
Him: (becoming animated) we were playing on hard ground yesterday so the ball was quick-
Me: (interrupting in a desperate attempt to head him off at the pass) Did you get hit on the knee by a cricket ball?
Him: (ignoring me) I was batting sticky-leg-before-wicket-straight-on (this is just a rough translation, you understand) and I'd just clipped the ball on the outside of my bat-
Me: So you got hit on the knee by a cricket ball?
Him: Smithy was running the crease on the left hand side of the leg-over googlie and the Umpire was biased because he's only got one eye. Jonesy was giving their team a bit of rag which was a bit out of order when I was 99 for 56 in the fifth division league of gentlemen...
Me: (desperately) My ears are bleeding...
Him: (oblivious) yaddah yaddah yaddah cricket...blah blah blah... sixer... scoreboard bat...
Me: Please stop talking!
Him: and the ball glanced off the outside of my knee
Me: So you got hit on the leg with a cricket ball.
Him: Yes

Dear reader, before you write with outrage that I am a mean and uncaring wife who takes no interest in her husband's sporting career – you are right. I have tried, truly, to a) understand cricket and b) give a flying fig about it, but it just isn't in me. Just because we are married, doesn't mean we're joined at the hip. You could equally argue that since I glaze over at the first syllable of crick-, he really shouldn't inflict these details on me. Or that I should be more blatant than saying "Please stop talking" as that is too subtle a hint, but it wouldn't have any effect. Husband of my heart clearly derives pleasure from talking about his exploits on the cricket pitch whether I am listening or not.

Today, I am going to be driving for five hours with him in the car. I asked him, this morning as I taxied him into the office, "please don't criticise my driving every five minutes on the journey – I find it stressful and you might find it painful when I thump you."

He took that opportunity to list all my perceived driving faults, in detail, with specific examples. I could feel my blood pressure rising, the vein in my temple started to throb and I had a vicious urge to punch his bruised knee (caused by being hit by a cricket ball, don't you know?)

So, darling, if you're reading this, I'm going to put it in black and white: I have been driving for 32 years. I have had fewer accidents than you. I have incurred fewer speeding tickets than you. I drive myself all over the country, generally without incident or upset. If you trust me to deliver us to our destination safely, then keep *schtum*. If you don't, then drive yourself. Either way, I am begging you, publicly – please don't criticise my driving. Or talk about cricket. Or rugby. Or ANYTHING else that involves a bloody ball.

A MATTER OF IMPORTANCE

Today I have been preoccupied with a question of grave importance. It has involved me in considerable heart-searching, involving time and effort and consulting with others. It is not a matter to be taken lightly, nor is it something that one has to contemplate every day. It has, in short, been exhausting.

What, I have asked myself, am I going to wear to my party? (You didn't know I could be this shallow, did you, huh?) All you fashionistas out there – look away now.

Thing is, I don't do dresses as a rule. My legs only come out at the swimming baths: I live and work in trousers (mostly jeans). Not that there's anything particularly wrong with my legs, you understand, I just prefer clothes that let me leap around without flashing my knickers. Women's clothing is so bloomin' impractical (even trousers don't have enough pockets). Not only do skirts and dresses allow unfortunate draughts to tickle one's undercarriage, they require the wearing of tights or stockings.

Well, you can forget the stockings – bloody ridiculous fastenings – and as for tights, who in the name of Pretty Polly invented those? Assuming you can get a pair to fit you (no mean task – one size? ha bloody ha) a second pair of underpants worn over the top is necessary to stop them rolling over the belly and creeping to mid-thigh, thus acting as a hobbler. (a friend of mine – who shall remain nameless for obvious reasons – was shooting a wedding recently and had to nip behind a pew to peel hers off mid-ceremony).

I could go bare-legged, of course, but bearing in mind

129

that my legs see the light of day so rarely, you can imagine the luminescence of my bluish-white skin. There isn't enough fake tan in the Midlands to rectify this state of affairs. Nor wax – omg, I don't think I can face it!

And on to the shoe situation. Can someone please explain to me why would anyone want to walk around on mini stilts all day? I know, I know – heels make the legs and *derriere* look more sexy, taking small steps makes a woman look helpless and sexually appealing, *yada yada yada*. I'm far too busy to think about looking sexy all the time. (Or at all, if I'm honest). I have places to go, things to do. Shoes are made for walking (and running) in, not for displaying my (not inconsiderable) assets.

Oh dear – do I sound awfully grumpy? It's this dressing up malarky – it makes me feel impatient. There's just so much fuss involved. You might like to know that I DID buy a dress, AND the appropriate undergarments. I drew the line at the Playtex 18 hour girdle – lifts and separates all day long. I want to be able to breathe. And move. Can you imagine wearing such a thing all day?

I know that many of you reading this will be spluttering into your coffee. I do try, honestly I do. Ask my daughters. They were both subjected to a barrage of picture text messages – what about this one? Too much cleavage? Good colour? Does my nose look big in this? – oh yes, modern technology means that I can shop with my girls even when they are miles away!

The upshot is that I shall appear at my birthday party looking as if I have made the requisite effort and, for one night only, my legs will be making an exclusive public appearance. Then they'll disappear back into my jeans, where they belong.

2018 Note: This post was accompanied by a small barrage of support from regular female readers:

Kim said: *Oh Jo, I love the way you articulate, your post really made me smile ! As long as you feel comfy that's really all that matters, if you have had the ok from your girls then worry not, daughters are the best critic !! Don't forget to exfoliate the legs and be liberal with the moisturiser....don't go for the cross your heart brassiere if one cares to sport a cleavage.....do have a splendid party and enjoy 'yourself'. Kim* xx

"The Wartime Housewife" (google her blog - it's fabulous!) had this to say: *Gosh, I'd never thought about wearing a second pair of pants over my tights – isn't that just asking for a disconcerting fungal infection? At least you'd never get sexually assaulted, it'd be like throwing cucumbers at a trampoline. The thing with high heels is you have to practice wearing them. As a youth I wore stilettos every day and I could actually run in them. Then I moved to the country and lived in Doc Martens and comfy sandals so I could run after my toddlers, and now I've trained myself back into high heels. I never mince in them, I stride out manfully – er – womanfully. Make the distinction between heels you can actually walk in and shoes that are only for lying down in! If you're wearing a low cut dress, I heartily recommend going to The Little Big Bra shop in Market Harborough and getting fitted for a really sexy one. It will do wonders for your honkers and will feel gorgeously comfortable as well. Thus spake the Wartime Housewife!"*

Gilly also had words of encouragement for me (plus lots of exclamation marks!): "*oh yes...I am with you fully....jeans jeans jeans... in the Carib it was short shorts shorts. I own one dress that I bought for a special occasion one year to take back to the Carib should I be invited somewhere that needed such a garment. I wore it 7 months later to my own wedding, thank you Mc&S!...Enjoy your evening in your dress, I know when you put it on you will feel a million $$$$$$$$$$$$$$$'S, I did! Looking forward to seeing the photos of your special day....oh and your birthday !!!!!!!!!!"*

Me*: Thanks for your comments, girls! I would like it to be known that I am not acquainted with any "disconcerting fungal infections", nor have I any experience in "throwing cucumbers at a trampoline" lol!* xxx

131

50 WAYS TO FLOURISH AT 50
Numbers 26-30

An "empty nest" can be re-feathered to suit the two of you.
Or can be sold to downsize and release some fun-money.

"Fun" is not a dirty word and the young do not have a monopoly on it.

If you're single, remember that you're never too old to fall in love.

If you're not, now is the time to re-ignite the love that burns quietly for your long-term partner.

Make a point of listening to new music every now and then. Nothing is better designed to make you feel old than realising a whole new genre has passed you by. Bonus: there's bound to be someone/something new that you actually like!

CHAMPION

I made a mistake the other evening. How? By challenging son no 1 to a game of Scrabble. I used to be good at Scrabble. I liked playing (because I was good). Dammit, it was me that taught him to play. Here's how it went:

Him: 26 points

Me: 15.

Him: 68 (he used all 7 letters)

Me: zero (I had to miss a turn to exchange my entire rack)

Him: 64 (he used all 7 letters)

Me: 16 (he placed my letters for me because I couldn't see a single opportunity and he got fed up with waiting)

Him: 35

... you get the gist. On his seventh turn the score was 261 vs 86 and I lost the will to continue. It's no fun when you're that far behind, is it? I can't do Sudoku either. Or crosswords. (Though I can mutter cross words while I'm trying).

Does it matter? I wish I could say "it's the taking part that counts" but, dammit, I'm just not feeling that sentiment!

Son No. 1 was crowing all evening about taking my title as family scrabble champion. Actually, there are two things wrong with that sentence: 1 – he wasn't crowing, more like smirking quietly, and 2 – I never was the family Scrabble champion.

I just remembered that.

ON REALITY

Reality is merely an illusion, albeit a very persistent one.

(Einstein)

He was a clever fella, that Einstein, wasn't he? I've been pondering the above statement for a while. What did he mean? That we all live in some Matrix-style fantasy, or that he was partial to the odd tab of LSD? (Just kidding, legal protectors of Mr Einstein's reputation).

When I was a kid of 8 or 9 I remember asking my mum, how do we know that we're really here? She answered with a clip round the ear (that was allowed in those days) and I remember thinking, well, I felt that so this must be real.

Both my sons are prone to metaphysical speculation. It made for some fun conversations around the dinner table when they were young.

If a tree falls down in a forest, did it really fall down if nobody saw it?

What makes you think reality depends on human perception?

So if I leave my vegetables on my plate, did I eat them really?

eh?

Just because you didn't see me eat them, doesn't mean I didn't.

But they're there on your plate still.
Are they? Isn't that just your perception of reality?
Eat your vegetables.
But they don't exist!
Eat your vegetables or I'll clip you round the ear.
I'll phone Childline!

How times change!

Eleanor Roosevelt said no one can make you feel inferior without your consent which is a tacit acknowledgement that we can affect our own reality. However storm-tossed our little boats might be on the turbulent seas of life, we can always control our own reactions. We can choose to be battered, or choose to be the quiet, calm centre at the eye of the storm. So when all around you is chaos, close your eyes and find your own reality.

SCARIFICATION

...is that even a word? I've been scheduling the last few posts of project50 in it's current format and I have to confess to feeling rather sad. I'm not going to go away completely, but nonetheless, it's the end of something that has turned out to be significant to me. I fear I am going to miss you.

I've been cleaning a lot too. So much so that daughter no.1 phoned her dad the other day. Is Mum all right? she said, allegedly. She's fine – why? Husband of my heart enquired, oblivious. Well, every time I speak to her lately she's cleaning the house...

I suppose I want to step into the next part of my life with everything in order. Does it sound as if I've lost my mind? I do wonder whether Sunday is going to be an incredible anti-climax.

Anyone would think I was getting married, or emigrating. I suppose I am, in a way – emigrating to the other side of 50. I need to get a wriggle on and get my new projects underway or I'm going to be bereft. Bereft AND 50. Now there's a scary thought...

LETTER TO YOU

Dear Reader,

(By which I mean you – yes, you in front of the computer screen… stop looking behind you… I'm talking to YOU…) One year ago I started writing this blog, not knowing whether anyone would want to read it, feeling very much alone in my ambivalence about turning 50. Twelve months, 346 posts, over 600 comments and more than 15,000 views later, and life feels very different to me.

Life is a bit like hill walking – you're following the path, but the view keeps changing. This **project50** year has seen me climb up, up, up from the valleys, walk around a corner and stop to say WOW! There's a whole new vista laid out before me, and it is breathtaking.

Some of you have been walking alongside me, via comments on the blog and emails. You have allowed me to interview you, sent me funny pictures and ideas for articles. Some of you have told me you have been inspired to make changes: Karen has started her own business, Sally began to look after herself and think about what she wants from her life and Jill is counting down to her 50th birthday in May 2012 by writing her own blog to celebrate her *"Year of Jubilee"*. I have had regular correspondence with two readers who have been through some dark times and, in turn, I have been encouraged, comforted and inspired by regular commenters such as Old Fool and The Wartime Housewife.

My own life has been a bed of roses over the past twelve months – particularly thorny   roses! Life has been

– and continues to be – testing at times and occasionally even heart-breaking. I have learned that opening one's heart can mean becoming vulnerable to being stabbed in it.

I am learning to shield myself just enough to resist the urge to retreat to a safer place, for the good far, far outweighs the bad. Kurt Cobain once said I would rather be hated for who I am than loved for who I am not (note to Nirvana fans: I realise I've probably paraphrased that!)

Some of my virtual friends have become friends in "real" life. Some of my family tell me they have got to know me through the blog and we have become closer as a result. That says a lot about my purpose in writing it: I wanted to marry the person I was on the inside with my public persona. I'm still working on that. A lifetime of staying in the background, of being inoffensive – and insignificant – is not easily overcome. One thing is sure, though – you haven't heard the last of me! I am far, far happier for being true to myself and for standing up to be counted.

Now, my chicks are all heading for the nest today and I need to go and make up the beds. I'll see you tomorrow!

AFTER THE PARTY

I am in Norway, overlooking the Sognefjord. For some reason, the words I am typing on my new iPad (so much more exciting than diamonds and fast becoming this girl's best friend!) are not   appearing on the screen in front of me, so I am typing blind. For that reason, I'll keep this short!

Thank you for all your goodwill messages for my birthday last Saturday. On Saturday night, almost every person I love in the world were gathered together under one roof. That was the best birthday present I could ever have had.

We danced the night away to the Rockabilly sounds of the Hounddogs, three brothers who don't just play their instruments, they rock them. The day after the party, those of us who remained went out for Sunday lunch and Husband of my heart presented me with tickets for a West End show *Million Dollar Quartet* – an imaginary reconstruction of the night in December 1956 when Johnny Cash, Carl Perkins, Jerry Lee Lewis and Elvis Presley all came together for an impromptu jam session at Sun Studios. It was a wonderful, light-hearted show – and I was able to give the dress a second airing!

I woke up in the hotel the next morning to find that son no 2 had lugged suitcases to the hotel two days before which had been hidden, unbeknownst to me, in a wardrobe. My case had been lovingly packed by my husband with an eclectic selection of mismatched clothes, most of which had been in a pile ready for the charity shop. My dismay soon turned into excitement as I realised that I was about to fulfill item no.1 on my bucket list: we were flying to Norway. That lunchtime. Secretly, I've always wanted to be "whisked" somewhere!

I have never been so thoroughly and delightfully surprised as I have over the past two weeks. Thank you to everyone who made it happen. Being 50 is fabulous!

50 WAYS TO FLOURISH AT 50
31-35

Embrace new technology. We all know the cliche of the grandparents who had to ask the   grandchildren to set the video to record for them. If you make the effort to upgrade your phone, keep up with the way we watch TV, browse the internet etc now you won't get left behind as you age, feeling baffled and helpless.

Buy non-stick pans. Life is too short to spend scrubbing porridge-encrusted saucepans!

Smile. No matter how bad life gets, there's always something - or someone - to smile at.

Laugh often. What else can you do? Especially when you take off your bra. Or your underpants.

Never close the door on an idea that enthrals you.
If you've always wanted to try belly dancing, or learn the piano, or visit Venice for *Carnivale*
DO IT.
Why not? What's stopping you? If not now, when?

THEY COME, THEY GO

I seem to spend a great deal of time greeting and good-bying in my hallway (hey – I made up a verb!) I'm finally learning to take each day as it comes and live in the moment. I think it was John Lennon who said that life is something that happens when you're looking for something else. At the end of the day, that's what life is, isn't it – the moments that make up our days and weeks and years?

Life has ensured that Son no.1 has learned that lesson early – one small bonus in a life-changing upheaval. I watch him make the most of every second he spends with his children and find myself hoping for that state of grace to spill into other areas of his life.

We learn so much from our children. I find myself continually (and by turns) inspired, exasperated, filled with pride, humbled, awed, supported, consumed by anxiety and infused with joy by mine. (No wonder I'm so bloody tired!)

I've spent too much of my life trying to bend myself into shapes to conform to imagined norms. When I gave up work to care for them in those early years, I fretted that I wasn't earning, nor living up to my feminist principles. When I was writing through the night I felt guilty that half my mind was composing stories while I was in the park with the kids.

If I have one regret about my time as a mum, it's that I allowed anxiety – about real things such as how we were

147

going to pay the mortgage and my daughters' health, and imagined things, like "*what ifs*" and "*am I good enoughs*" - to take my mind away from the moment I was in. I see young parents with their kids in the park staring at their mobile phones and I want to shake them and say: you have a lifetime to talk on the phone – be here now with these little people that need you. They'll be gone soon enough.

Now, at fifty, I no longer have time for regret. I'm learning to slow myself down at points during the day to consciously immerse myself in what I am doing, and to give my attention to the person I am with.

Years ago, my grandmother sent me this little poem, cut carefully out of the letters page of a women's magazine. I'm afraid I don't know who wrote it. My husband subsequently had it written out and framed and it hung, (not entirely unheeded, as anyone who visited the chaos that was my home at that time will testify) on my wall for years. I would like to see a copy inserted into those little packs they give new mothers in hospitals. Maybe fathers could have it tattooed up their arms.

I hope when my children look back on today

They remember a mother who had time to play

There will be years for cleaning and cooking

Children grow up when you're not looking

So quiet down cobwebs, dust go to sleep:

I'm rocking my baby, and babies don't keep.

IN PRAISE OF FATHERS

I am 50 years old and I still miss my dad. I wrote about him last October on the anniversary of his passing. The truth is, you never really lose a parent. Love them or loathe them, they live on in memory, in our hearts, and in the little voices we hear in our heads: *you can do it!...you're useless...I'm disappointed in you...I'm so proud...*

Yesterday we lost a relative who was a father and grandfather, pushing my husband and his cousins to the top of that particular family tree. We are now, effectively, the elders.

As I sent my condolences and informed the younger members of our branch of the family, that cold feeling I carried around after Dad left us tickled at my heart. To know you will never feel again the safety of a father's arms around you, or smell that familiar, reassuring scent of him – these are things for which there are no words of comfort.

A good father is there to throw you in the air when you are small, to pick you up when you fall, to tell you that you are beautiful, or strong, or whatever it is you need to hear. A good father sets boundaries for us to make us feel safe, guides us and protects us and is prepared to fight for us to his last breath if necessary. I hope that my father, and the father who left this world yesterday, knew that they had done their job, and were proud. For we are all proud of them.

I TAKE MY HUSBAND FOR GRANTED

… and he does me, but I would argue that that is a VERY GOOD THING. Allow me to explain.

When I married him, 30 years ago today, it was with the intention of spending today celebrating our 30th wedding anniversary together. Ok, not this day specifically, but you get my drift. Last year, I wrote him a letter here on the blog, so if you've been with me since then you probably know how I feel about him. Over the years, I've noticed that I only ever really think about our relationship when we're out of tune with each other. Most of the time, it's a fact of life.

We're like Morecombe and Wise, cheese and biscuits, Fred and Ginger (but without the dancing). He's the Tonto to my Lone Ranger, the wind beneath my wings, my anchor in a storm.

To paraphrase WH Auden (shame on me!), He is my North, my South, my East and West, My working week and my Sunday rest, My noon, my midnight, my talk, my song. In a word, he is my husband. It might be old fashioned to say this, but I am proud to be his wife.

Now, I know that some of you are thinking that I am being naive (or even smug). True, there's time yet for him to have a mid-life crisis and run off with some floozie. To fancy a beefburger when there's steak at home. He'd find it difficult, mind, after he's been "bobbited" (I keep a pair of rusty nail scissors on standby, just in case such surgery is required). But what's the point of worrying about that? We're happy now, today, and you know what? That's enough.

Our marriage isn't just about him and me. A wedding is the beginning of a family. The vows we made are set in stone as far as I am concerned (I wouldn't mind a bit of the "for richer" though now please, dear.) They are sacred, the closest thing I have ever come to holy.

He supports all my wild ideas, both practically and emotionally. He knows me well enough to know he should never tell me not to do something. In turn, I barely batted an eyelid when he came home from work to me and our (then) three little children and announced he was going to set up on his own. We have each other's backs, and even during the times when we don't get on so well, we are a team.

It works, I think, because we have a system. He cooks; I eat. He makes money; I spend it. I talk; he watches the cricket.

So you see, being taken for granted is not necessarily a bad thing. To know that your partner in life trusts you implicitly to be there for them through thick and thin, to hold your heart gently in their hands and to help you to breathe life into your dreams, gives you a warm feeling inside. To be trusted to that extent is a blessing. To walk through life with someone you, in turn, trust equally in that way is divine. That, to me, is "for richer", and the greatest hope I have for my children is that they will each find someone whose love and support they can take for granted too.

I had a notion that I wanted to mark our anniversary by renewing our vows, but Husband of my heart was of the opinion that the old ones haven't worn out yet. So we'll be spending the day quietly together (because, obviously, we don't have much to say to each other after 30 years! – *boom-tish!*)

So, in the words of the great Slim Whitman: *Darling, Happy Anniversary-eee, another year of love has gone by. Thank you for each day you give to me -eee, my darling Happy Anniversary!*

Is now a good time to mention I forgot to buy you a card?

SWEET AND SOUR

I was chatting to a young friend on Facebook the other day who is about to have her second baby, and she mentioned how angry and frustrated she gets when her grandmother gives her little boy sweets and biscuits. Ah, I told her, you're talking to the wrong person – I'm guilty as charged – I really do have to reign myself in when it comes to offering sweet treats to my grandies.

I explained to my friend that feeding the little boy sugar was probably the way her grandmother showed her love. It got me thinking – when we were small sweets and chocolate were rationed – not in a "during the war" kind of way – I'm not that old! – but certainly they were saved for... well, rewards and treats.

One of my earliest memories is of my grandmother, with whom I lived at the time, scooping up a fingerful of butter from the butter dish on the table, dipping it in the sugar bowl and popping it into my mouth. It makes me feel quite sick to think of it now, but it remains in my memory as an association not only with her, but the feeling of being loved. Powerful stuff, psychologically.

Remember, people weren't as effusive with their hugs or their praise back in the 50's and 60's – we weren't far away from the "spare the rod, spoil the child" philosophy of child rearing. An approving look, a kiss or a cuddle were jewels to be treasured from our grandparents. It wasn't that they didn't love us, they just showed it differently. One of the ways they showed it was with sweets.

One of my grandmothers never visited without boiled sweets ("acid drops", as I recall) in her voluminous handbag, another baked cakes. When my own children came along, I always had a chocolate bar in the car when I picked them up from school (until we worked out we could go on holiday with the money if we gave them up!)

So if any young parents are reading this, don't be too hard on your parents and grandparents – we don't mean to undermine you. Telling us not to buy your children confectionary is like telling us we are not allowed to show our love. It really isn't about sugar and calories. Point it out to us, and we'll realise, hopefully. And if we don't, take comfort from the fact that your children, brought up on apples and raisins, will more than likely say "no thank you" to our wilder excesses in any case.

A PERFECT DAY

Husband of my heart saw Santa yesterday, so now his year is complete. Not that he needed his belief reinforcing by meeting the great man, but you could tell that inside his boots, his toes were curled with excitement as we queued. Husband, that is, not Santa.

Santa appeared a little discombobulated by an account of a grown man's good deeds and asked him how old he was. "53", he replied, "and-"

"Actually," interrupted the eldest of our three grandsons, "Grandad has been very naughty. He teases me all the time." There was a second's silence in the grotto.

"But I'm a Grandad – that's my job!"

Santa smiled sagely. "Let's take Grandad out of the equation for now, shall we? What's your name? And are you on my good list?"

And so back to Son no 1's flat to decorate the tree. He wasn't going to bother, being a bit *bah humbug* about Christmas in general, but luckily his eldest son was having none of it. Banging on the Christmas music, he and his little brother danced around the room, the baby looking on and kicking his little legs in delight. Then they looped Christmas stars and baubles round the branches until even Daddy was compelled to don a Christmas hat and dance a jig. That's the thing with Christmas: it gets to us all in the end.

After weeks of feeling under the weather, spending those few precious hours with my husband, son and grandchildren was just the tonic I needed. Being a grandmother is one of the greatest gifts life has given me and one of the greatest compensations for growing older. They live too far away for me to be with them as often as I would like, but it gives me endless joy to see their faces light up when I walk in the room. And since my son doesn't allow me to bring sweets, (see earlier post!) I know they really are pleased to see me, not just the contents of my handbag!

The middle one is at the stage where he repeats the end of everything you say: "Do you want to hang the Christmas star," "Christmas Star", "That's a tricky one!" "Tricky one." So I decided to see how far it would go and said: "That was serendipitous!" He paused for a moment, looked me straight in the eye and said, "yes, Grandma."

We travelled home last night to our evenly decorated tree and I felt quite sad. It's not so long ago that ours was bottom heavy and leaned slightly drunkenly to one side like our son's. I always resisted the urge to rearrange it beyond making it stable after the children had gone to bed – it wouldn't have been the same if I did and I'd hate to think of them noticing and thinking they hadn't done it "right". I think I might put on the Christmas CD this evening and spend a little time dis-arranging ours, just for old time's sake.

50 WAYS TO FLOURISH AT 50
Numbers 36-40

Cultivate curiosity. Who knows what new experiences
you'll enjoy, who you might meet,
where you might go if you just keep curious?

Always treasure your capacity for empathy.
Empathy and compassion are what make us human.

Step outside of your comfort zone regularly.
Even small things - like taking a different route home,
speaking to someone unfamiliar, trying a new activity - if
they make you uncomfortable then,
once conquered, they will make you stronger.
Then you can challenge yourself to do more exciting
things...

Never apologise for yourself. Who you are needs no
excuses. Unless, of course, you are morally or criminally
aberrant. In which case I'm assuming you won't have time
to be reading this.

Never waste time worrying about what other people think
of you.
You don't have time for that any more.
Besides, what others think about you is none of your
damn business.

ADOS: Attention Deficient Ooo Shiny!

On my way home to Northamptonshire from Bath last night, I was diverted onto the M48 because the Severn Bridge was closed to traffic due to high winds.

UK readers will know there are several things wrong with that statement. For a start, Wales is not usually on my itinerary – clearly I took the wrong turning onto the M4 and, in the driving rain, failed to notice the absence of Swindon. (I was wearing the glasses prescribed to stop me falling asleep as well). 45 minutes into my journey later, I passed my original motorway entry point and, quite honestly, passed the point of no return.

I have posted before about my failing mind, and many of you have been kind enough to jump in with words of reassurance and sympathy, which is nice, especially since Husband of my heart can only point out that I am a liability.

I put it down to a momentary lapse of concentration. Unfortunately, several moments quickly add up to a permanent state of bewilderment which is, I have to admit, a bit of a worry. I blame the government. Just kidding. I do blame our attention deficient society though, which has made the act of concentration a dying art.

Son No. 2 has ADD – Attention Deficiency Disorder – or "a creative brain" as we call it, depending on how annoying he gets. At school it was a problem as there was always something more interesting going on in his head than what was happening in the room. In the real world, it makes employment in regular jobs a nightmare. He once worked as a waiter and couldn't remember an order from table to kitchen. But it also gives him the most incredible powers of concentration when he is engaged with something, such as writing music.

The older I get, the more I find myself drifting off when uninterested. Maybe I'm just turning into a cantankerous old git who can't be bothered to be polite any more. Perhaps I should buy a SatNav, except I really don't like being told what to do.

I could do with a cyber-hug from you if you have the time. I'm feeling a bit worn out today. Sometimes, I think it's best just to give in and have a duvet day when you have a flat battery, don't you?

A SHARED HISTORY

I am both blessed (and cursed) with two younger sisters. Every year, we say we are going to make more effort to get together. This year, we actually made a January meet-up and spent last night in the cinema (watching Meryl Streep's version of Margaret Thatcher).

As they chatted in the bar (over cappuccinos in polystyrene cups – oh yum!) I realised that these girls, 5 and 7 years younger than me, are getting older. I say "they chatted" because I find it difficult to get a word in edgeways. It was ever thus – in our house, she (or he) who shouted loudest and talked the fastest got the most attention and I never did have the energy to compete, preferring to bury my nose in a book ("stop wasting your time reading, Jo, and do something useful!" – Hang on – how did Mum get in here?)

Anyways, they were talking about their various aches and pains and the latest new diets embarked upon. And I thought, you know what, if we had been sitting here last year, or five years ago, or ten, we would probably be having the same conversation. That's the thing about sisters – love em or loathe them, they are part of your history.

I just read back over the preceding paragraphs and realised the tone could be read as quite tetchy. So I ought to say right here, right now, that I love my sisters, that I actually wouldn't change them for the world, and that now we are all getting older, I really would like us to sustain the effort to see each other once a month!

I am so grateful to have them in my life. They are a

constant. Like my brother, they were at my 50th birthday party, along with their families. They have been at almost every family celebration, helping with the food, washing up, burning up the dance floor, showing that they might not always like me, but they love me, just as I do them. That's a pretty powerful certainty to carry through life and forms part of my bedrock.

These women are strong, funny, talented and loyal. They have each faced life's ups and downs with fortitude and grace, being there for each other through cancer, divorce, loss and struggle, yet they can still sit quite happily and discuss, at length and in detail, exactly what they had to eat today and whether their bowels are working properly.

Because that's what sisters do – they bring you back down to earth. You know they remember you as a scrawny kid with her head in the clouds, and will have no hesitation of reminding you of that fact should they ever deem it necessary. And by the same token, they are at the front of the crowd when it comes to applause and encouragement. So here's to my sisters - may they never change.

AN ATTITUDE OF GRATITUDE

It's a funny old world in which we live at the moment, isn't it? I don't think I know one person who isn't struggling with something, whether it be financial, emotional, physical or spiritual. Perhaps it's just that people don't tend to seek you out and tell you that they're really happy and life is going extraordinarily well. Maybe we should: "Hi Jo – just thought I'd call and share my contentment with you." It's ok – go on: you can do it!

Seriously, I think the whole world is out of sorts at the moment, and I am no exception. Changing one's life and making things happen isn't always a bed of roses, you know. Self doubt still stalks me, and I'm still all too easily diverted from my purpose by anxiety, or by worrying about my children and their various (and varied) crises. The point is, it's not what happens to you in life that counts, it's how you deal with it. Every morning, I get out of bed and, on some level, I make a choice. Most days I choose to be happy.

Today I am simply grateful to get by. Because some days, that just has to be enough.

FRIENDS

Thick or thin, (the times that is, not the friends!) there have been people there for me over the past couple of years who have variously:

planned

shared

laughed

cared

cried

grieved

comforted

believed

chivvied

commiserated

applauded

celebrated

supported

shoved

helped

loved

You know who you are. "They" say that some people are in your life for a season, some for a reason, some for life. I have learned over the years that that's ok – friends can come and go, our relationships are no less valuable. Others become family. I am just thankful that my circle of friends has expanded to include so many talented, kind and giving men and women. And I look forward to meeting many, many more.

THE FUTURE CAME LAST MONDAY

I woke up on Monday and realised the future had arrived.

It might have been the drugs, of course, but it was a pretty cool feeling, I can tell you!

Perhaps I should explain about the drugs. Last Friday I had a shoulder arthroscopy and capsular release – i.e: I had my frozen shoulder fixed – under general anaesthetic, and have been on industrial strength pain killers ever since. That means I feel no pain. And I mean NO PAIN.

As anyone will know who has suffered with any chronic physical problem, you don't actually realise how much it was affecting you until it's fixed. Does that explain the huge surge of physical energy I experienced in the week after the op? Or the glorious mental clarity? Maybe it was a morphine-high. All I know is that I've spring-cleaned the house, have almost finished my annual accounts and suddenly feel quietly confident about the direction in which I should take my business. Best of all, I feel calm. And happy.

Husband of my heart keeps looking at me sideways, as if half expecting me to have collapsed into a tearful heap. My physio has had a rant because I've spent the first week of my convalescence with a wet cloth in one hand and a vacuum in the other. I don't care – I feel marvellous (and my house is clean). The future is here – and I like it!

THE FUTURE WAS A LIAR

Last week I posted about the massive high I experienced after my operation, and shared with you my concern that it might be the drugs that caused it. I've calmed down a little since then, and, guess what? I've discovered that it was indeed a side effect of a massive dose of steroids injected into my shoulder. Bugger.

I'm told it will be around in my system for a good 3-6 months, nestling in my liver etc, but that the good stuff I experienced last week was probably a flash in the pan. What a shame – I really liked that feeling of energy and clarity. In fact, I hadn't realised how befuddled I have become until the kenalog whooshed through my brain, clearing away all the cobwebs.

I had a long chat with my GP about the ageing brain. I know I'm not alone in finding a loss of mental clarity – a decreased ability to concentrate and variable moods – one of the most   irritating and unpleasant developments as I get older. My doctor tells me it might pass. Or it might not. She tells me that no, it isn't possible to have an implant of kenalog to provide a constant drip drip drip of the good stuff (why not? I pay my taxes!) and she pointed out that if I carried on at   energy level I was at last week, I'd probably have collapsed by now.

Just one question: why oh why did I waste   wonderful surge of energy cleaning? For pity's sake – I could have written a book or finished researching the family tree or something –   anything – that lasts longer than a shiny bathroom. Oh well. Back to normality then. At least the sun is shining!

HELLO, GORGEOUS!

Well, that's what Husband of my heart was supposed to say after I'd had my make-up "done" by an "expert" recently. What I actually got was silence and a look almost of fear in his eyes. Which was puzzling as I thought it looked quite good. Then I put my glasses on and checked myself out in the car mirror and – OMG!

You see, I don't generally wear much "slap". I'm a pass my fingers through my hair, put on some lipstick and run kinda gal. (OK, as I've got older I've added "fill in my fading eyebrows and dab a bit of foundation on the broken veins" to that routine, but that's a bit wordy, isn't it? Loses impact.) I feel I need to look a bit more "groomed" though – apparently research has shown that women who wear make up earn more than their bare-faced sisters and lord knows I could do with a bit more cash. So I thought I'd have myself "updated".

Anyway, the girl I was talking to on the make up counter looked impressively dewy, so I trusted her to make me up with a light touch. Only she had to do something else, so she went to find a colleague. The second girl was a slightly alarming shade of orange, was wearing false lashes and had eyebrows that were a work of art. I could hardly back out when I saw her though, could I? What would I say? *Sorry, but I don't want to look like you, darlin'*?

So, a good half an hour later and I was concealed, foundationed, powdered, bronzed, blushed. My eyes had been outlined, contoured, highlighted, mascara'ed and my brows "defined". They felt heavy and when I opened them wide the lids stuck briefly to my lower brow. My lips were so sticky I felt as if I'd eaten a whole sachet of sherbet dib-dab but, as I say, the mirror reflected a pretty "groomed" woman, so I was happy.

"It makes you look flat," said Husband of my heart. "Everything that makes you 'you' has been ironed out." What? Freckles, wrinkles, broken veins… is that the sum total of what I have become? Then I put on my glasses, looked in the mirror and saw how the foundation was caking over my chin, how my eyeballs looked slightly yellow against the eyeshadow and my eyebrows gave me a slightly quizzical, demonic air.

"She's made your eyes look worse," he said, getting into his stride. Worse? *Worse?* I didn't know they were "bad" in the first place! "Your crow's feet are deeper." Okay, I have to concede he had a point, but what woman wouldn't sulk a little at that remark? It's almost as bad as telling me a top I was trying on "Made me look good from the front." Oh yes, that's another of his gems.

So, I went home and washed it all off. Thing is, that girl made me up the way she would make up a 20 year old. It's not her fault, she doesn't know any better. No one has taught her that older skin reacts differently, or that more mature eyes need a lighter touch. All the magazines she reads and the conversations she hears are probably about older women wanting to look younger.

I don't. Honestly. I've done 15, 25, and 35 and 45. I don't want to cover up the age I am – I just want to look like the best version of me. What does that mean? Well, to me it means smoothing out my skin tone, defining a little the features that have faded and adding a little colour. It doesn't mean obliterating what my husband calls my "natural beauty". (Sometimes he actually says the right thing.)

Now I'm off to wash my face, run my fingers through my hair and add a dab of lipstick   before I dash out of the door…

A LAMENT

I was making soup.

I forgot I was making soup.

I have no soup.

And no pan.

FLOW

Do you ever get so engrossed in what you're doing that every part of you, mentally, physically and probably spiritually, is engaged and time ceases to have any meaning? Everything is falling into place, your ideas are coming together seamlessly and your productivity, (though you're probably barely aware of this until later) soars. The house could start to burn down around you and you'd still "just finish this bit". If you do, you know the true meaning of "flow".

If this doesn't resonate with you, watch a child play by himself. Immersed in his imagination, his whole body will be involved in what he is doing. We tend to lose such intense focus as we move out of childhood. So the child who could spend days at a time in a fantasy world of her own making will gradually lose the ability to escape the mundane, and the necessary skill of being in the here and now subjugates the need to dream.

Well, yesterday, I was "in flow". It was one of those wonderful "I love my life" days. It started, as most do, with a walk in the beautiful countryside that surrounds me. Full of sunshine and fresh air, I came home feeling inspired and was soon in that glorious state where one idea triggers another which leads to another and, rather than disappear into the ether as so often they are wont to do, they all found their way onto paper. People I needed to contact to progress these ideas were all in when I messaged or called, everyone I spoke to was available and willing to get on board, Husband of my Heart was playing cricket, so the

175

house was quiet and, because I knew he had dinner planned, I was able to survive the day by foraging through his chocolate store (I mean, who leaves half-eaten chocolate bars lying around in drawers?)

Imagine my distress, then, when the doorbell went. On a Sunday. It was the fish man, wanting to restock our freezer.

"I'll have a box of mixed white fish," I said immediately, remembering that's what we'd had before.

"I've got some lovely sea bass on board, fresh as you like, beautiful it is – come and have a look."

Bearing in mind I'd already taken off my glasses, which had interrupted my flow (who can flow out of focus, I ask you?) I obliged by shoving my bare feet into my slippers and grabbing a coat. It was bloody freezing outside, more so when I stood by the open doors of the refrigerated van. The fish man started to unload his stock, box by box onto a trolley.

"We've got some smashing prawns – look at these. Fresh from Icelandic waters."

"Very nice, thanks, but I'll just have the mixed box." Hurry up, I wanted to say, I need to get back to my desk.

"How about some Norwegian salmon – line caught, no farmed stuff. They eat their own droppings in those pens, you know." They did look good and we do eat a lot of salmon, droppings and all.

"We do chicken now, pre-prepared…"

I could feel my flow ebbing away. "Thanks, but I'll just have the fish."

"These are seasoned with -" could have been nettle needles wafted with witch's breath for all I know, I'd stopped listening, desperately trying to hold on to my previous train of thought.

He went on and on and on…and on. He's a very nice man and I didn't want to hurt his feelings. But nor did I want him to unpack his entire load and show me the contents of virtually every box as he worked his way to the elusive box of mixed white fish, right at the back, at the bottom.

Allow me to cut what has already been a very long story short(er). I ended up buying four boxes of fish instead of the one. Roughly fifty pieces of mixed white, sea bass, tuna and salmon. I filled in a pre-signed cheque that I happened to have in a drawer that Neil left me a year or so or go that I never used. I vaguely heard the phrase "discount for bulk" but my mind was already back indoors, in the warm, on my project.

I was still "flowing" when Husband of my heart came in from cricket. "I bought some fish," I told him happily, "hope that's OK. It was £190."

The penny dropped as I said it aloud. OMG. I had spent £190. One. Hundred. and Ninety. Pounds. On fish.

He looked at me. I looked at him, dismayed. Without a word, (bless him for his restraint) he went off to cook chicken for tea. I have a feeling that's the last time we'll be having meat in this house for a while...

Have a good week. I hope you get to "go with flow" – flow is good. Just learn from me and don't make any buying decisions while you're in it!

50 WAYS TO FLOURISH AT 50
Numbers 41-45

You are now an elder (yes - you!) As an elder, take seriously your responsibility
to nurture the young, help them in their careers when you can, and pass on your values.

Cultivate an "attitude of gratitude". Bored at work? Focus on being grateful for the living it gives you. Noticed another grey hair? Be grateful you have lived long enough to grow old!

Attitude is King. Sometimes we can't control the things happening around us,
all we can control is our reaction to it.

Accept, finally, that the one thing we can truly rely upon is that nothing ever stays
the same and learn to embrace change.

Resolve to say "yes" more to the things you want, and "no"
to those things that make you feel less.

TRAVEL TIPS

Having spent a wonderful few days in Barcelona with Daughter Number 2, I've been preoccupied with travel tips for those who are, like me, in possession of 50 year-old legs. Mine, you see, are currently worn down to stumps. And swollen. Not to mention the fact that my back feels as if it's been snapped and I could happily sleep for 24 hours straight. Allow me to impart my hard-won wisdom on the subject of travelling with someone much younger than oneself...

1. When booking a cheap hotel for a city break, check first where the red light district is located. Our room was clean and comfortable, but overlooked a street that was, um... lively all day until about 4am. This didn't seem to bother my daughter, who slept like a log, but I seemed to be party to every negotiation. Fortunately, I don't speak the language, or I might have been tempted to lean out of the window and yell: just pay her already, you cheapskate!

2. Take two pairs of comfortable shoes and alternate them. Forget heels – you'll never keep up, never mind look elegant.

3. Either wear clothes with secure pockets, or put your valuables in a small bag worn across the body and under your jacket. That way your bag can't be snatched, pick pocketed, or cut from you with a knife wielded from a passing moped. (We had no problems like this, thank goodness, but we made it difficult which I think helped)

4. Following on from above, walk in the centre of the pavement and keep your wits about you. Check your route before you leave the hotel and if you have to check a map or phone, duck into a doorway or a shop and be discreet. Don't wander around in a dream with your iPad in your hand...

5. Insist on being fed and watered regularly and keep hydrated throughout the day.

6. A siesta is a cultural experience in Mediterranean countries. Return to the hotel and make the most of it by lying down with you feet higher than your heart. Be prepared to listen to music so that your companion doesn't get bored and hustle you off again before you've recharged. I was lucky – my young person slept for longer than I did.

7. Make a lose itinerary, plan your route and don't waste your leg

power wandering around looking for things. Make the most of the underground system and buses. Consider hopping on one of those tourist buses so that you get a quick overview of the sights whilst sitting on your butt, giving you an idea of those you'll want to visit later.

8. Further to the above, consider climbing to the highest point (normally in a park or up the tower of a cathedral) on the first day so that you get an overview of the city. That way you won't feel overwhelmed by the endless concrete throughways that you have to navigate to find those pretty squares and narrow streets.

9. To save weight, download a travel guide to your smartphone BEFORE you leave home. Leave it until you get there and you'll end up burning through your 50megs for £40 by using data roaming.

10. Don't be afraid to slow things down if the pace gets too much for you. There's a lot to be said for pacing, for sitting in a cafe and watching the world go by and using the time to chat and reconnect.

My lovely girl is off again tomorrow having been home for just 10 days. Those four days in Barcelona were so precious – and worth every ache, blister and sleepless night!

DON'T SCARE THE HORSES!

Have I ever mentioned how much I love my job? But it ain't always easy. Take yesterday. Off I go to capture another *50 Facing 50* volunteer. Kit ready, break in the rain, shoulder holding up. So far so good. Find the village, then the house, no problem, arrive on time.

Yvonne is lovely: kettle on, dressed ready for the shoot, raring to go. So we shoot a couple of quick portraits, talk about what we were aiming for and head off to the paddock. Yep – the paddock. Did I mention I'm scared of horses?

To be honest, I'd all but forgotten myself – it's been a while since I tried to ride one. That occasion led to me having to be lifted from the back by a young man with well-developed biceps because my hips froze into "astride" position and I couldn't swing a leg over to dismount. I might have told you... But I digress...

Striding into the field after Yvonne to meet Andy and his two grazing companions, a little voice says in the back of my head: "Blimey, they're a bit bloody BIG! They've spotted me... they're coming towards me... they're ALL coming towards me... now they're trotting.... SH*T!!!!!!!!! What do I do now?"

"Are you nervous of horses?" asks my host as she catches sight of my face.

"A little bit," says a small, strangled voice that seems to be coming from my throat.

"Just stand still – they're coming to say hello."

I'd rather they didn't, to be honest – I'd be happy with a polite nod from across the way, but I can hardly outrun them, can I? Especially not with a camera and lens bag slung across my shoulders.

I woman up, let them snort and sniff around me and try to pat one nonchalantly on the nose. It nips me. It hurts. Is that a precursor to trampling? Or eating? I turn my attention to Yvonne, who is trying to persuade Andy away from the sweet new grass. I've decided to use a long lens, (surprise, surprise!) which Andy suddenly finds fascinating, so he trots up to have a closer look...

I start to relax a little once we move into the paddock away from the other horses. I have a shot in mind that I'd really like to capture, but apart from that, I go with the flow, forget my fear and roll happily around in the fresh, wet sheep droppings... Ok, that's a lie. I kneel in it and grimace, roll in it and squeal like a little girl and eye the sheep (who have ridiculously long, curly, pointy-tipped horns) with distrust.

Andy is a character, though, and I have to confess I rather like him by the time we've finished. I swear he even winks at me once, but that could just be the relief of having survived the shoot...

I'm a country girl until it comes to non-human living things. Then I turn into a city girl complete with the metaphorical inappropriate footwear. Loved the shoot though. And if you ever need an equine photographer... I can put you in touch with a couple of experts!

CONTENTMENT

I'm typing this from my sofa on a rainy Sunday afternoon. Husband of my heart has popped out to buy milk for a cup of tea and some cake, (I hope!). My study has been commandeered by son no 2 who is busy producing a new track he's co-written with Billy Lockett. I can hear the same snippet of the same song being played over and over again as he makes the track richer by adding strings, drums, layer by layer.

Half an hour ago the three of us were out walking in the lush green fields nearby. We were rained on once but, as Billy Connolly would say, there's no such thing as bad weather, only the wrong clothing. Most of the time, the sun shone as we variously strolled and chatted or marched in companionable silence to a soundtrack of birdsong. We came together, now we've moved apart to each our own thing. Later, we'll come together again to sit round the table for dinner which Dan will cook, it being Father's Day.

Son no 1 and two of our grandsons Skyped this morning. Daughter No1 rang before her shift at the museum. Daughter No2 will probably call when she finishes work at the pub. According to her Facebook status update, she has another tattoo, so that will no doubt form part of her conversation with her dad.

Family life changes as the children grow up and leave home, but it's always there to be enjoyed by whichever one might drift home. I feel a quiet inner peace today, which I will savour. I think what I'm trying to say is that, as a society, we can spend too much time deciding what constitutes happiness, or functionality when it comes to families. Like so many things, it's up to each of us to find a way to be together that suits us.

My tea and cake have now arrived – my life is complete!

TO RUN THE RACE

Today I want to share something small but amazing – I won a medal! Me, Jo-always-bring-up-the-rear-at-school-sports, with a bum so big it's always running a metre behind and trying to catch up, came first in a race!

Ok, so I should admit to a couple of caveats here. I was in the the 5km walking group and, strictly speaking, Husband of my heart let me cross the finish line before him.

I'd like to be able to tell you that it was a breeze, that the me that was creaky, achy, fat (to be frank) who couldn't run up the stairs and suffering frequent, rather worrying chest pains when this blog began two years ago, broke into a run every now and again. I can't tell you that. The unvarnished truth is that I'd been on my feet for 10 hours the day before photographing a wedding and my knees protested for a full three days afterwards, but it's a start.

I can, actually, run for 20 minutes on a treadmill these days, but I've never tried running outside. Maybe next year I will enter the 5k again and attempt to run it. After all, I sure can walk fast now!

THE IMPORTANCE OF FAILURE

Not as in failure to post for over a week – apologies for that if anyone missed me! Between you and me, I've been feeling a little tired and discouraged (don't tell anyone – I need to keep up appearances). No, I've been mulling over the role of failure in both creative and business endeavour (not the whole time I've been away, you understand!). Fear of it paralyses so many of us. We have a great idea, then fail to act on it because we're scared we'll fail and end up not doing anything at all.

I meet a lot of people with brilliant ideas. In fact, was talking to someone just the other day who has a really interesting creative idea. She described it to me in some detail and I could see how it could work. She'd obviously spent a great deal of time and energy thinking it through and was enthused by the idea.

"Of course," she concluded, "it probably won't work."

"Why do you say that?" I challenged her, having just privately concluded the opposite.

She shrugged, and listed several obstacles in her way. I picked up each one and made her consider how they could individually be overcome. Will she press forward with her idea? I don't know. Sometimes it's easier to remain in the ideas stage, comforted by the possibility of success than take things forward and risk having that optimism taken away.

I met someone the other day who used to attend a writing group to which I belonged when I was published regularly. She used to turn up every month with the same idea – one book she was itching to write, but never quite finished. As you might have guessed, she still hasn't finished it – but it's still ongoing. Fear of exposing her magnum opus to the world and seeing it fail has meant it will probably never see the light of day, and she will never feel failure – nor the glow of success. If only she could recognise that that particular idea is a lame duck she could move on to something else. For as long as she holds onto it, fresh ideas will be blocked. The willingness to fail is a prerequisite to succeeding at anything.

Son no.1 plays a strategy card game in which he is known as a good "deck builder". He tells me he produces dozens of unworkable decks, but that if he didn't keep putting them out there, he'd never produce gold. I admire him for recognising that at such a young age. He knows that he has to put aside fear of ridicule in order to grab glory and that sometimes you have to pick through a lot of dross to find that nugget of gold.

I have to take some rubbish pictures in order to progress. If I don't experiment, I know I'll get stale and complacent. I have to try new things before I know whether they will work and not be afraid to "waste" my energy. For experimentation is never a waste, particularly when it comes to creative endeavour. You have to keep the wheels oiled, the brain ticking over and be willing to take a circuitous route. And, just as importantly, you have to be prepared to let go.

When I worked in the job centre, I spent hours in the evenings developing an idea I had to bring together skilled job seekers with unemployed school leavers. Ultimately, I concluded that the blocks to making that idea happen were too great – not least that I realised I really didn't want to run this company. It's a shame that I couldn't pass my idea on to someone who could have made it happen. It was a good idea, and I had to work it through or it would still be crawling around in the back of my mind, blocking more workable ideas.

Anyway, I've probably rambled on for long enough. If

you're still with me, you probably have the stamina to see your ideas through! Watching the Gymnastics heats at the Olympics I can't help but imagine the number of hours spent in repetitive training to get to the level of an Olympian. That's what driving forward, not being afraid to fall off the barre, figuratively speaking, means. Embrace failure and you have the chance to succeed. Fear it, and you'll stay where you are.

Right, I'm off to run on a treadmill. Staring my fear of failure right in the face!

ON SUCCESS

Yep, I'm still on a ramble! After writing about the importance of failure, I've been meditating on the nature of success. It was regular **project50** commentator, Oldfool who set me off on this train of thought. Below is the unedited comment he posted on my last post:

"In my short life (73+ years) I have compiled several lists of failures. Several because of the different categories, e.g. love, business, etc. Seems the score is about even up except that overall I am satisfied so perhaps I did better than I thought. I am happy to say that I have learned from my failures and not repeated them. I have tried the same endeavors over again using different inputs. I have never feared failure but neither does a cat which is why you occasionally see a flat dead cat in the road. When I say I cannot do something it is based on having a failure not on the lack of trying. My feelings about writing is that I am a success. Not because I'm good because I know 'good' and I ain't it. It is because it makes me happier and sometimes gives me a real sense of satisfaction."

I agree – failure is only useful if one learns from it! But what, then, is success? Oldfool says he feels he is a success at writing because it makes him happier. I like that. No mention of it   making him richer (financially) or that it "makes a difference". Just that it makes him happy.

I believe that success is something we all have to define for ourselves. What does it mean to you? Climbing the career ladder? Or being able to work part time so that you can pick your grandchild up from school? One is not more valid than the other, both are forms of success.

What signifies success to you? Money in the bank? (or even in your pocket!) A stable relationship? The ability to get up in the morning and face the day with optimism?

Here's what it means to me, for better or worse. While it would be nice to have the earning power to help my children more, in reality success, for me, is to be able to earn enough money at what I do to be able to continue doing it. To have the ability to be absorbed in my endeavours so that my attention is fully on creating, not paying the bills. Success involves maintaining a state of emotional equilibrium so that I can operate within parameters that are comfortable for me. To be able to spend time with my family, time with my husband, time with my friends, and time alone without feeling I'm being pulled every which way. In essence, I'm with Oldfool on this one. Success isn't about worldly renown, it's about doing the things that make me happy.

On the other hand, I would welcome the kind of success that sees book sales rocket and more and more quality bookings in my diary because, professionally, that is what success is all about. Isn't it? Validation of one's efforts. Proof that people want and enjoy one's output. And that has to include some monetary reward.

In conclusion, then, I'm pretty conflicted about what success means to me. I guess it's a patchwork quilt of things both big and small that bring me satisfaction. How about you?

LETTER TO MY DAUGHTER ON HER WEDDING DAY

Dear K,

So here we are on the eve of your wedding – your last day as a Blackwell. Tomorrow you will make the biggest commitment of your life so far and all your family and friends will gather together to witness the vows that you – and Frank – are about to make.

The day is yours, but your marriage belongs also to family and society at large, for a wedding is not just about the joining together of two people, but the beginning of a family unit. Whether that remains the two of you, or whether you are blessed with children, I know that you both will take that responsibility seriously.

He's a nice chap, that Frank. To be honest (I daren't say to be frank!) I was a little concerned at first, knowing that you're likely to remain as poor as church mice for the foreseeable future. Your tastes have always run more to Tiffany and Moet rather than Walmart and beer – in other words you have what my nan used to call a "Champagne taste on a beer income".

But I see the way he looks at you, I have watched how he has cared for you and loved you, and I see the difference that love has made to you and I know you are both wealthy in all the ways that matter. Plus I am actually quite fond of him.

Dad will be making a speech tomorrow. Ominously, it's all in his head and he won't discuss it. So I thought I'd say what I want to say here. After 31 years I think I can claim to be reasonably knowledgeable about marriage. So here, for you, and any young woman reading, is my checklist for a happy marriage.

- Always, always, be kind. Kindness is a grossly underrated virtue. If you can love him in spite of his faults, and forgive him when he messes up (as, inevitably, we all do at times) and treat him with gentleness and understanding, you will continue to grow closer, year on year.

- Never lose your ability to empathise. This follows on from the first point, but can't be emphasised enough. Recently, I asked an elderly gentleman how he and his wife had stayed married for more than 50 years. This is what he said: "If she always puts you first, and you always put her first, you can't go wrong. It's not rocket science."

- Hang in there when times are bad. Chances are you will fall in love with each other again, and if you give up, you will never know. In a long marriage you will, inevitably, have ups and downs. Remember, love is like the tide – it ebbs and flows. When times are bad, it's your friendship that will get you through, so never neglect it.

- Let him be a man. This is an important one. In today's society, men tend to be held up for ridicule far more often than they are praised. As a man, he has attributes that are different to, but that complement yours. Allow him to do things his way and in his own time or you will spend half your life nagging.

- Stay in touch with your girlfriends. Much as you love him, he will never be able to use as many words in a day as you. It's not the way men are made and you will get frustrated with him if you sense he's not listening. It's a wild generalisation, I know, but most women process things by talking them through, most men go quiet.

- Put him first. This might seem to contradict the previous point, and echo the second, but what I mean is, you are now a unit and no one should ever be allowed to come between you. Obviously, there will be times when it is only right that one of you will step aside to give the other space to put someone else first, but generally he needs to be confident that he is your priority, as you are his. I hope I will always be an important person in your life, but I now happily and gracefully (I hope – might cry a bit tomorrow!) step aside and take my proper place in your lives.

- Be wrong sometimes. In the few moments when I was alone with my dad before we left for the church, he offered me these words of wisdom, which I pass on to you in his memory: "Jo, you're always right. You know that. I know that. But if you want to be happily married, sometimes you have to pretend to be wrong." I laughed at the time, but over the years I've come to realise what he meant. Sometimes, you have to let go of the need to prove yourself right and just choose to be happy.

That's about it really. Take the time tomorrow to breathe and enjoy the perfect day you have planned so carefully. And step into this new chapter of your life with a spring in

your step and a light heart – there is no better way to live than with someone you love, who loves you, by your side. Good luck, my darling, and may all that you wish for yourselves come to pass.
Love always,
Mum xxx.

2018 Note: *This was one of the most popular posts on project50 in terms of views, striking a chord with many readers judging from the emails I received recounting personal stories that often resonated both with pride and ambivalence at the prospect of "letting go" of a daughter.*

...AND SHE'S GONE

In Bangkok. With Chang. Not dead.

That's the Facebook status my daughter posted this afternoon. Who's Chang? I asked, fearing she had been inadvertently been recruited as a mule on the flight over. Beer came the response. So that's all right then.

It's not as if she isn't street-wise. She's been travelling alone since she was 16 – Amsterdam in the winter. That first trip was a baptism of fire since her flight was delayed overnight, she got on the wrong train in Holland and – survived. At 19 she backpacked across the USA alone. She knows what she's doing and I don't generally worry that much, once she's gone. It's the going I find hard.

The sofa seems awfully empty after two month's occupation. It's not that she's noisy, (though the TV is!) It's just that she has this huge energy that fills the house with...something energetic.

It's weirdly quiet today and- hang on... Son no 2 just rocked up with singer/songwriter and friend, Billy Lockett... they've gone into my garage – sorry – music room and fired up the keyboard. The kick drum has started up and...wait for it... there's the guitar.

Different kind of energy, but it's life, Jim, just as we know it.

You do know by now, don't you, that I write these posts as much for myself as for you? That I don't actually have any answers, I just pose endless questions. Questions to which there probably are no answers, but that bother me nonetheless. Like: did the midwife really cut the umbilical cord when these people were born? Or is there actually an invisible, mental cord, or a heart string maybe – a chord - that keeps them close in my heart and mind even when, physically they aren't here?

I know women who are able to simply move on themselves when the kids move out – or move out themselves! Others who move home, meaning that all that's left for their offspring is a sofa to kip on when they visit. I'm not saying that's wrong, I just know from my own experience how much that can hurt.

It's a standing joke between me and son no2 that he can only imagine me in relation to himself. So when I hear his key in the lock, I wake, like clockwork and become "Mum" again.

Silly boy. Silly me. I spent last Saturday helping daughter no1 and her husband move house. I'll visit son no1 and the grandies this Saturday. And in between I'll sort out my marketing plan for my business and maybe do some Christmas shopping. Maybe even see husband of my heart for a while. I need a life. I have a life. I'll make a new one.

Just not today. Today I miss someone. And I feel a little bit lost. Think I'll go and get me some Chang.

TIS THE SEASON...

...to remember what a klutz I am. Sellotape and me, we don't get on. I forget this, it not being a   particularly interesting fact, and always tackle the Christmas wrapping with gay abandon. I mean - how hard can it be?

I've noticed over recent years, what with the trend towards old fashioned values and the resurgence of "craft" and hand-made goods, that present wrapping has almost become a competitive sport. Beautiful paper - for which, more often, read "wholesome brown paper hand-stamped with potato cuts sculpted into snowflakes" - and elaborately tied ribbon or raffia, or hand-stitched tagliatelle (I made the last one up) have become de rigeur. How a gift is wrapped has become more important than what's inside. It tells the recipient how much you care, how much thought has gone into the present. What do you make of this lot then, family & friends of mine?

That's right - I can't cut in a straight line for toffee. And Sellotape is OUT TO GET ME! I swear. I take my time and think it through. I fold the paper carefully around the gift and lay the scissors on the fold while I pull out a strip of sticky tape and... need the scissors to cut it, so replace scissors with knee. Then I realise I'm in danger of losing the end of the tape - someone shoot me now! - so I stick the strip I've cut off onto the edge of the sofa leg (can't use the table - it's covered in presents waiting to be wrapped) and carefully fold over the end.

So far so good. The paper is still neatly folded under my knee, the strip of sticky stuff is waiting to be applied...to my fingers. It's wrapped itself around my fingers so tightly that I have to use the scissors (with my left hand) to free myself. I start again, only this time before I get it onto the paper one end decides to mate with the other and I'm left with a Sellotape porno-loop. The next attempt adheres to the carpet and is too furry to reuse. Finally, I manage to hold a strip of Sellotape at either end, position it over the fold, remove my knee and NOOOOOOO! It's touched the wrong part of the paper and is now attached, uselessly, across the front of the parcel.

Ffs! It's enough to make a saint swear! I can feel my Christmas spirit receding as I prepare to start all over again... only I forgot to fold last time and now I can't find the end. I can't see it. I can't even feel it. And I've put my finger through the paper, so I'm going to have to patch it up. With tape.

At least I've bought the effing Sellotape, and all the wrapping paper in time this year. When the kids were small we always ended up wrapping late on Christmas Eve. One year we had to resort to cutting up magazines and scrabbling around for old newspapers to use as wrap. On one memorable occasion, Husband of my heart realised he'd left a sack of presents at the office and had to go back to fetch them in the wee small hours of Christmas morning. Ho ho ho.

My wrapping skills didn't matter much when they were young - the paper was ripped off so quickly in their excitement at seeing what was inside. Sadly, I am now exposed for what I am - a domestic failure. A woman who allows herself to be bullied by a roll of sticky tape. Good job they love me, eh? Hang on - I left all the parcels in neat little piles according to whose were whose so that when I found the gift tags I could label them... why are they suddenly in a heap all together? Now I can't remember what's in each parcel, or who the lucky recipient should be. Dilemma - do I start again, or shall we have a "lucky dip" Christmas?

LETTER TO MY FUTURE SELF

Hey Jo!

How does 60 look? Or 2021 for that matter! Is there still a Eurozone? Has the global economy settled? Is George Clooney still hot?

Obviously, I can't know what has happened to you in the ten years after I write this, but using now as a starting point, I'm going to make what I hope is an educated guess and project into the future. I'm hoping that you no longer sit and write blogs like this at 3am because your brain is so busy it won't let you stay asleep. Ergo you're not exhausted a lot of the time – all that exercise and stretching and healthy eating has paid off and you're fitter and lighter on your feet than you ever were in your 30s and 40s, and full of health and energy.

You've learned to pace yourself, of course, and to listen to your body. You take the rest you need and embrace it as you embrace everything in your life now. It wasn't until you were in your late 40s that you were able to walk into a room and have the expectation that you're welcome there. That was a huge breakthrough, having spent much of your life until then feeling as if you were in the way. Now that you're 60, you've moved on a level and don't actually give a shit – in the nicest possible way, people can take you or leave you. How liberating is that?

I can't imagine that you've lost your love of

connecting with people though, and you'll have found a way to be of service without compromising yourself and your own needs. I imagine it includes photography and writing, because you've no thoughts of retiring yet, have you? Maybe you're able to be selective about the assignments you undertake, but so long as there are stories out there to be told that interest and excite you, why would you stop? Besides, after a dozen or more years of practice, I guess you're pretty good now, aren't you? A few exhibitions under your belt, healthy sales securing a residual income for your retirement, when it comes? Oh good – that is a relief from my perspective here!

Tell me – you didn't need to expend so much worry on those you love, did you? They all turned out ok, didn't they? You've been there when they've needed you, of course. But once you realised that the greatest gift you could give your children was the knowledge that you loved and trusted them enough to work things out for themselves, that freed you to put all that mis-directed energy into your passions, paving the way for the most creative and productive decade of your life so far. How does it feel, to have shed that cloak of constant anxiety? I can see how much lighter you are, and not just physically. I'm so proud of you for stepping into the light!

You always knew that things can change in the blink of an eye, that all you had to do was let go…and breathe! So simple, yet so hard to accomplish when all around you is chaos. The more you "tried" to let go, the tighter you clung on… ironic, isn't it? That we "strive" to relax?

Yet now I can see you are breathing easily. Still the fulcrum of your family, but no longer the anxious, neurotic matriarch. Surrounded by your children and grandchildren, happy still with Husband of our heart, fulfilled in your work now that you can let your creativity have full reign – there's not so big a leap between you and me, is there?

Ten years – so much living to be done between where I am now and where you are. I can see from your face that, looking back at me you trust me to take the right path. So

I'm going to start breathing – now, today. I'm going to let go of all that anxiety and fear that weighs me down. Because, looking at you, I can see that I have no use for it, it serves no purpose except to hold me back.

Right – I'm going back to bed now. It's 4.30am and I need my sleep. There's nothing to keep me awake now I've met you/me ten years from now – I KNOW that everything and everyone is going to be just fine: including me!

NEW YEAR, NEW OPPORTUNITIES

I LOVE New Years. Just as I love the first empty page in a new notebook – all that pristine promise! It doesn't matter how banal my thoughts might be, I just know they will reach new levels of profundity in a new notebook! No matter how difficult, or tiring the dying year might have been, the next twelve months are spread out before us like pearls on a necklace, all shiny and precious, just waiting for us to wear them to the party. (see – profound, right?)

Life's certainties - we're born, we get older, we pay taxes, we die - are taken for granted. It's the grey areas we so often have trouble with – how will we spend those years we have on earth? Will we be loved? Have a passion that enthuses us? What storms will batter us and can we withstand them?

We know really that, of course, we will, even if we think we can't. What choice is there, after all? We make choices when we open our eyes every morning (and not just the "shall I get up now?" variety). We choose whether to be happy. Whether to allow ourselves to bend, but not break. We choose whether to criticise or encourage, engage or ignore those around us, whether to coast along or strive to be better.

I'm not making resolutions this year – I've decided that the whole too fat, too thin, too unfit, too loud, too quiet, too *anything* just doesn't apply to me any more. I'm not perfect, but I'm ok. But I will spend a little time considering the choices I intend to make this year. And I wish YOU (yes, you) a happy, healthy, productive New Year!

50 WAYS TO FLOURISH AT 50
45-50

Don't compare yourself to others. Your journey is yours,
your achievements as valid as the next person's
no matter how "small" they might seem to you,
or in the greater context of society.

Now is the time to start being more gentle with yourself.

Stay interested in life - it is very interesting!
Keep looking outward,
stay open to the opportunity of change.

At 50 your life is almost over...or just beginning. You
choose.

In summary, to flourish in your fifties stay as fit as you are
able,
remain curious, keep your heart and mind open and
celebrate coming into your own.
50 is largely what you make it. It might as well be fabulous!

WHAT I WISH FOR MYSELF

I started this blogging journey with a long, long list of things I wanted to achieve at 50. Things like climbing the Norwegian Fjords, (not the actual fjords, of course – the rocks around them...what are they called? Cliffs?) visiting all the US states, losing a stone in weight etc etc. Well, I've achieved the first and last and there's no reason why I won't do all the other things that were on my Bucket List if I put my mind to it. However, I have learned so much about myself through writing his blog. My life has changed over the past two years, and so have my priorities.

What do I wish for myself now that I have passed that fiftieth birthday milestone? Here's my own personal Bucket List:

- I hope I stay curious. Curiosity is, in my opinion, one of the greatest attributes that a parent can nurture in a child and one of the greatest gifts we can give ourselves. It gives us the ability to stay interested in the world.

- I hope I stay fit and supple in both body and mind so I can enjoy the years ahead to the full.

- I am looking forward to making more and more portraits and finding new ways to share the beauty I see through my lens with the world.

- I wish to stay connected, and to be a useful part of my community.

- I will continue to watch the progress of my children and grandchildren with pride and wonder.

- I would like t spend mire time with my sisters and my brother.

- I want to sing, dance and drink champagne on a regular basis.

- I want to see more of the world and the people in it.

- I look forward to continuing to love my husband, for the rest of our days.

And that's it, really. I guess I've discovered that life is simple. It's about family, friends and community. It's about being useful. It's about having an open heart as well as an open mind. And I've realised that I'm ok. Which is really quite important.

I wish the same for each and every one of you (except for the loving my husband bit).

THE END OF THE BEGINNING

So there it is. The distilled wisdom of the people I met mixed with my own conclusions about this new stage in life. I have loved sharing this journey with my little **project50** community and I will miss writing the blog. I would recommend blogging to anyone who has something they want to share with others - we live in a world where we now have the facility to make our opinions known, where anyone can have an audience and where citizen politics is gaining ground.

For myself, I know that the time for thinking and agonising over growing older is done and the time for action has at last come. I need to just get on with it and I am looking forward to life's next adventures, whatever they might be!

WHAT HAPPENED NEXT?

Whilst I got on with living, questions about ageing and what it means to be a mature woman in today's society continued to interest me. My Portrait Photography clients are often women my age, many with similar concerns to those I had. I have also come to believe that the world needs our experience, knowledge and love.

That's why, in 2018, I have launched The Midlife Movement, a community of like-minded women who want to make the most of the next phase of their lives. Women who, like I did, have paused around the time of their fiftieth birthday and taken stock. Where have I been? Where am I now? Who am I? Am I happy? If not, what am I going to do about it?

The Midlife Movement is a resource for training, coaching, support and inspiration for creating change where required so that you can craft the life you want. It's the resource I wish I had been able to access at the time I was writing this blog.

I talked a lot about in the blog about stepping into my own space after years of supporting others. Ironically, I have now come full circle and embraced the facilitator in me!

Women thrive when they support each other and I love my Midlife Movement Community. I'd love for you to join us, both in our Facebook Group and as a Subscriber.

Thank you for buying this book. I hope you enjoy it. If you do, you might like to know that I've also started blogging again - every Friday at:

www.themidlifemovement.com

I'd love to see you there!

ABOUT THE AUTHOR

Jo Blackwell is a Portrait Photographer and Writer. Based in the UK, she travels extensively in the pursuit of interesting people to interview and photograph. A mother of four children and almost 6 grandchildren (to date!), she remains in a constant state of both worry and joy!

Jo is also the Founder of The Midlife Movement, an online, subscription based community which exists to help women create their best life in their midlife.

"Our Mission is to help Midlife women who want to do something good in the world step into their space with confidence and purpose, and have fun doing it!"

www.themidlifemovement.com

www.joblackwell.co.uk

Made in the USA
Monee, IL
09 January 2022